MUHAMMAD ALI

THE UNSEEN ARCHIVES

MUHAMMAD ALI

THE UNSEEN ARCHIVES

William Strathmore

Daily Mail

p

This is a Parragon Book
First published in 2001

Parragon
Queen Street House
4 Queen Street
Bath, BA1 1HE, UK

Produced by Atlantic Publishing
Designed by John Dunne Design
Origination by Croxons PrePress

A catalogue record for this book is available from the British Library.
ISBN 0 75256 008 5

Printed in China

CONTENTS

INTRODUCTION

The Greatest

uhammad Ali first came into the public eye when, as Cassius Clay, he won a gold medal at the Olympic Games in Rome in 1960. The gold medal winner became the golden boy of American sports. In 1964 he stunned the boxing community with his defeat of Sonny Liston, the heavyweight champion, and then shocked the world when he announced he had become a Muslim and changed his name to Muhammad Ali immediately after the contest.

When he refused to go to fight in Vietnam because of his beliefs he was branded a draft-dodger and threatened with prison. The boxing authorities stripped him of his title and he was effectively banned from fighting for over three years; the golden boy had turned into an enemy of the state.

Despite this, he stuck to his principles and during the years of exile from the sport he found a new life, spending time studying his religion and making a living from public speaking. Whatever people may have thought of him, it was evident that he was sincere in his beliefs and he started to reclaim the respect of the public, especially as his views on the war in Vietnam began to become more widely shared. At the age of twenty-eight and after the years barred from the sport he loved, he was able to resume his boxing career. He regained his title and went on to win many of the most breathtaking and memorable fights the world has ever seen.

During his career, his influence on the world of boxing changed the sport forever. He took the world heavyweight championship away from its traditional New York venue and made it a truly global event, fighting bouts in Canada, Britain, Germany, Zaire, Malaysia and Manila, as well as the United States. Before his fights he turned the previously staid ritual of the weigh-in into a performance of confidence and showmanship.

Using his position to speak out against inequality, and the money that he earned to help those less fortunate than himself, he came to have an audience that spread far beyond the world of sport. He became respected both as an ambassador for his religion and as a force for good who continues to try to give people hope.

In its nine informative chapters this book charts the life of this fascinating and complex man through a series of amazing action photographs, as well as powerful and intimate images of Muhammad Ali at rest or on the public stage. There are pictures, drawn from the Daily Mail's comprehensive archive, of Ali's major fights: from Henry Cooper to Joe Frazier, to his title matches around the globe. While the images shot during the fights show the raw power, athleticism and skill of the fighter they are balanced by portrayals of his humanity and wit. The pictures are accompanied by detailed and perceptive captions which add context and depth to give a rounded and comprehensive portrait of the man who truly is 'The Greatest'.

ACKNOWLEDGEMENTS

The photographs and supporting captions from this book are from the archives of the *Daily Mail*. Additional photographs to complete this fabulous celebration of the life of Muhammed Ali have been provided by the Hulton Getty Picture Collection.

Particular thanks to Steve Torrington, Dave Sheppard, Brian Jackson, Alan Pinnock, Paul Rossiter without whose help this book would not have been possible.

Thanks also to
John Anderson Christine Hoy, John Dunne, Cliff Salter, Richard Betts,
Peter Wright, Trevor Bunting, Simon Taylor and Frances Hill.

MUHAMMAD ALI

THE UNSEEN ARCHIVES

Chapter One

'I'm The Greatest'

f it hadn't been for a stolen bicycle, the world might never have known Muhammad Ali. In October 1954, 12-year-old Cassius Marcellus Clay - as he then was - rode his new bike to the Louisville Home Show at Columbia Auditorium. He and a friend spent the day there, looking round and picking up free samples of the food being exhibited, but when it was time to go home Clay realized that his bike was missing. He was directed down to the basement gym where Joe Martin, a local policeman, was teaching young boys how to fight in his spare time. Martin never found the missing bike, but he encouraged Clay to join the gym and start learning how to box. Six weeks later, Clay won his first fight - three rounds against another novice. He had discovered a natural talent and he worked hard to develop it, devoting his energies almost exclusively to boxing. By the time he was 18 he had already fought 108 amateur bouts, winning six Kentucky Golden Gloves championships, two National Golden Glove tournaments and two National Amateur Athletic Union titles.

In 1960, Clay was selected for the Rome Olympics, although at first he was very reluctant to go because of a fear of flying - a fear that remained with him for many years. In Italy he trained hard, but also found time to make friends and became one of the best-known and best-liked athletes in the Olympic Village. He won his first three fights relatively easily, but in the finals he was up against a much more experienced fighter - Zbigniew Pietrzykowski from Poland, a three-time European champion and a bronze medallist from the 1956 Olympics. Not only that, but the Pole was also a southpaw, which initially confused Clay. In the first round he took some heavy punishment, but in the second he managed to keep out of trouble. By the third he had found his form, and he ripped into the now-tiring Pole to win on points.

When Clay returned to America as an Olympic gold medallist and a national hero, he was pursued by managers and promoters eager to sign him. He chose a local syndicate, the Louisville Sponsoring Group, eleven men who came together to launch his professional career. They soon decided that a more experienced trainer was needed, and sent Clay to California to train with a living legend - Archie Moore. Unfortunately this arrangement was not a success. Moore tried to teach Clay a different style of punching and insisted he did his share of chores, but Clay didn't want to be told what to do and after less than two months he went home for Christmas and never came back. The search for a suitable trainer began again and this time the Louisville Sponsoring Group settled on Angelo Dundee, a highly respected coach who was based in Miami. Rather than pushing Clay, Dundee encouraged and directed him by praising his good points. The two of them quickly developed a lasting bond.

Over the next few months Clay fought several experienced boxers - and beat them all. None of them could cope with his speed in the ring, or with his taunting words during the fight, which often angered them so much that they forgot their technique. During this period he began to elevate his habit of 'mouthing off' into an art form. Until then, most fighters had tended to say very little before a fight but Clay changed all that. He was excellent at self-promotion and had the personality to carry off his outrageous claims. He was such a handsome, likeable character that what might have seemed unpleasant boasting was almost impossible to resent. He also began to recite poetry, composing rhymes predicting what he would do and making fun of the people he fought. One of the first poems was about winning the gold at the Olympic Games - on his return home to Louisville he recited it to the welcoming crowds at the airport. Another of his favourite ploys was to predict the round in which his opponent would be beaten. The first time he did this was in November 1961, when he announced that Willie Besmanoff would fall in round seven. Besmanoff was hopelessly outclassed and Clay could easily have finished him off sooner but he waited until round seven to make his prediction come true. The media loved it and began to focus their attention on him. This suited Clay, since he was always ready to promote his fights and could be relied upon for a good story. He was a charming man who was good company and many of the Press became friends, in particular Howard Bingham, a freelance photographer who worked for Life, Sports Illustrated and a host of other magazines. He and Clay first met in April 1962, when Bingham was assigned to cover the Press conference announcing the forthcoming fight between Clay and George Logan. Bingham went on to become Clay's closest and most reliable friend, supporting him when few others did.

By mid-1962, Clay had fought fifteen professional fights and had won them all. It was time to move on and fight a big name - and the name selected was Archie Moore, his old trainer. The up-and-coming champion was pitted against a renowned fighter - but Moore was now nearly fifty years old and past his best. The two of them were among boxing's greatest showmen and the battle of words before the fight was almost more exciting than the contest itself. Of course Clay won - and in round four, as he had forecast.

Seven of his previous eight fights had now ended in the predicted round and Clay had captured the imagination of the public. At his next appearance, at New York's Madison Square Garden against Doug Jones, expectations were running very high and the performance was sold out - despite a newspaper strike throughout the promotion period. However, things went badly wrong. Clay had predicted that Jones would fall in six, later adjusted to four, but he fought one of the worst fights of his life whereas Jones fought his best. It lasted ten rounds and Clay only just won on points. The fickle public turned against him and many influential sportswriters began to criticize his boasting and question his ability, so something had to be done quickly to regain his popularity.

As a result, Clay went to London for the first time to fight the reigning British heavyweight champion, Henry Cooper - a venture that almost ended in disaster. Clay had selected round five for Cooper to fall, and had made the customary statement to the Press. A barrage of jabs to Cooper's face soon had him torn and bleeding, but each time he was about to fall Clay would step back and dance around, determined to make good his prediction. Towards the end of round four Cooper summoned all his strength and let fly with his devastating left hook, 'Henry's Hammer', which connected solidly to the side of Clay's jaw and knocked him backwards into the ropes. A dazed and disorientated Clay managed to climb back up, stood for a second and then began to fall. But the bell saved him - in the confusion it sounded the end of the round and his handlers were able to rush forward and catch him. Clay was taken to his corner, but he was still stunned and in deep trouble. Dundee had noticed one glove was slightly torn earlier, but had decided it was not serious; now he quickly widened the split and brought it to the referee's attention. This ploy gained Clay an extra minute's rest to recuperate while a replacement glove was sought and he came out fighting. His first jab opened a cut above Cooper's eye and the following rain of blows nearly overwhelmed him. The referee soon stopped the fight.

Clay had now been boxing professionally for nearly four years and after eighteen fights he was still unbeaten. Despite this, there was some doubt in professional circles as to whether he could actually punch, and to fulfil his dream of becoming heavyweight champion of the world, he had still to beat the reigning champion, Sonny Liston.

Previous page: A publicity shot of the young Cassius Clay, taken early in his professional career.

Above: The Olympic champion. To the right of Clay is silver medal winner Z Pietrzykowski (Poland) and on the left are joint bronze medallists A Madigan (Australia) and G Sarandi (Italy).

Going for Gold

Above: A proud Cassius Clay stands to attention with his gold medal.

Right: Archie Moore winces as Clay lands a punch. Clay had predicted that he would beat Moore in round four and he proceeded to make good on his promise in front of 16,000 fans. Moore was a crafty and experienced boxer but he was no match for Clay's speed and strength. Minutes after the fight was over, Clay challenged the reigning heavyweight champion, Sonny Liston, but it was to be another 15 months before they met in the ring.

'It'll only go to five'

Above: Clay smiles and waves to his fans as he arrives in England in May 1963, three weeks before his scheduled bout against Britain's Henry Cooper. After having narrowly avoided defeat by Doug Jones in his last fight in New York, he was looking for a quick victory to restore his reputation.

Right: 'If Cooper whups me, I'll get down on my hands and knees, crawl across the ring and kiss his feet.' Clay holds up his hand to demonstrate that he will dispose of Cooper in round five. He had originally predicted round three, but amended it to five because he wanted the 50,000 fans who had bought tickets to get their money's worth.

Opposite: Before leaving America for London, Clay demonstrates his cooking skills by whipping up some pancake batter at home in Louisville, watched by his younger brother Rudolph.

The fist...

On Clay's arrival at Heathrow, Customs officials had
the temerity to ask him if he had anything to declare.
He immediately launched into a long oration on his
favourite topic - Cassius Marcellus Clay. It covered his
boxing skills, his beauty and predictions for the
forthcoming fight with Cooper. He finished by
demonstrating the fist that will knock Cooper down.

Opposite: The city gent. Clay gets into the spirit of
things for his stay in London.

After a short nap to recover from the long flight, Clay and fight promoter Jack Solomons leave the Piccadilly Hotel for a walk in the spring sunshine.

Right: Clay takes it on the chin from his youngest sparring partner.

I'm the prettiest

Right: 'I'm not only the world's greatest fighter, I am the world's prettiest fighter,' Clay tells the Press during lunch in a West End restaurant. He also revealed his ambition to have two chefs and two valets - so they could work shifts - a masseuse and a large apartment block as an investment to pay for it all.

Below: Jimmy Ellis, Jack Solomons and Henry Cooper laugh as Clay announces that he wants to fight Johansson, Brian London and Cooper in the same ring and that he'll beat them all in nine rounds. After someone pointed out that Johansson had announced his retirement that very day, Clay quickly quipped, 'He's smart!'

Opposite: Clay demonstrates the knockout punch again for photographers, along with raised hand to predict how many rounds the fight will last. 'Cooper goes in five... but if he pops off at me - it'll have to be three.' He also took the opportunity to have another dig at Liston, announcing that in his opinion, '...all heavyweights fighting today are bums and cripples - and that goes for that big ugly bear, Liston. He may be great, but he falls in eight.' Sports writers quickly dubbed him with a whole range of alliterative nicknames, including the Louisville Lip, the Kentucky Klaxon and the Garrulous Gladiator.

I'll give it five...

'Our 'Enery' shakes hands with his forthcoming opponent and slyly seems to make his own prediction of the result. Cooper was the reigning British heavyweight champion and a gallant fighter, but he was severely handicapped by a battle-scarred face that bled at pretty much the slightest blow. Clay, ranked 5th in the world heavyweight table, was confident that Cooper would be no problem to beat, but his arrogance was almost his downfall.

Introducing Cassius Clay...

Right: Cooper rolls up a napkin into a makeshift ear trumpet, all the better to hear Ali as he gets into his verbal stride during the West End lunch, which was given by Solomons to introduce the two fighters.

Below: Bud Flanagan and Jack Solomons crack up, but Clay can't seem to see the joke.

Opposite above: At Piccadilly Circus, Clay and his companion, Dave Edgar, stop to chat to a policeman. The previous day, Clay had announced he was too precious to sleep on his own in a big city like London, and had insisted that another bed be moved into his room for his bodyguard. He was already sharing the room with his brother, Rudolph, but a third bed was moved in.

Opposite below: On May 30, Clay was outside the ring for once, watching a boxing match in London. His fight with Cooper was still more than two weeks away and he had not yet got down to serious training.

Time to get down to some training...

Right: Clay finally begins some intensive training for the forthcoming fight with Cooper. Trainer Angelo Dundee laces Clay's gloves in preparation for a sparring session at the Territorial Army drill hall at White City, London.

Above: Clay and one of his sparring partners put in some ring work in front of an audience of invited guests.

Opposite: Clay adopts a fighting pose for the photographers in the run-up to the fight. Since this was the first time he had been to London there was a great deal of media interest in him. There were articles in the general papers as well as the sports Press - an early sign of him becoming someone of interest to a wider public, rather than just a sportsman. Columbia Records soon noticed this trend and only a few months later they released an LP, *The Greatest*, with Clay reciting monologues and poems about how great he was.

Family business

Above: One of Clay's sparring partners in London is his younger brother, Rudolph Arnette Clay, who was also a boxer, although he had not yet made his professional debut. The two brothers came from a closely knit family. When Clay started to become famous, Rudolph joined his entourage and usually travelled with him - first as his sparring partner and later as a companion and driver.

Right: Clay looks thoughtful as his gloves are laced for another sparring session.

Opposite: Clay bounces along Lower Regent Street with sparring partner Jimmy Ellis, on his way back from doing limbering-up exercises in Hyde Park. Clay completed four fast sprints in the park, impressing watching journalists with his fitness. The two of them had been up and out before 6 a.m. and had exchanged banter with bus drivers and cleaners who were on their way to work. As they jogged down the road the driver of a No 15 bus slowed down and shouted greetings. One of his passengers, an elderly woman, called out, 'Who are you?', to which Clay replied, 'I'm Sonny Liston.'

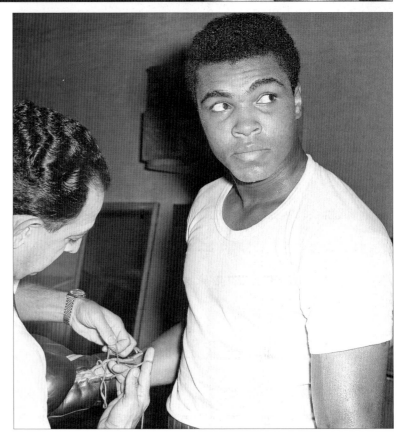

Cassius Clay
The Greatest

Above: Seated on the floor, Clay goes through a series of leg-
strengthening exercises. According to his contract with the
Louisville Sponsoring Group, he was due to receive 50% of the
earnings on his fights for the first four years, less 15%, which
was to be put aside in his pension fund. The sponsoring group
took the other 50%, but they paid for all the management,
training - including the trainer's salary - travel and promotion
expenses out of their half. The contract was considered very fair
and even generous for its time.

Right: At the weigh-in at the London Palladium at lunchtime on
the day of the fight, Clay and Henry Cooper are surrounded by
adjudicators. The event was open to members of the public and
the main part of the theatre was crammed with a mixture of
boxing fans, journalists and photographers, all waiting for the
final weight announcement.

Opposite: Clay's flamboyant, flaming-red, ankle-length dressing
gown had been tailored specially for him in London and had
cost the princely sum of UK£35. It was trimmed with a broad
band of white at the neck and wrists, with a white sash; the
wording on the back was also in white.

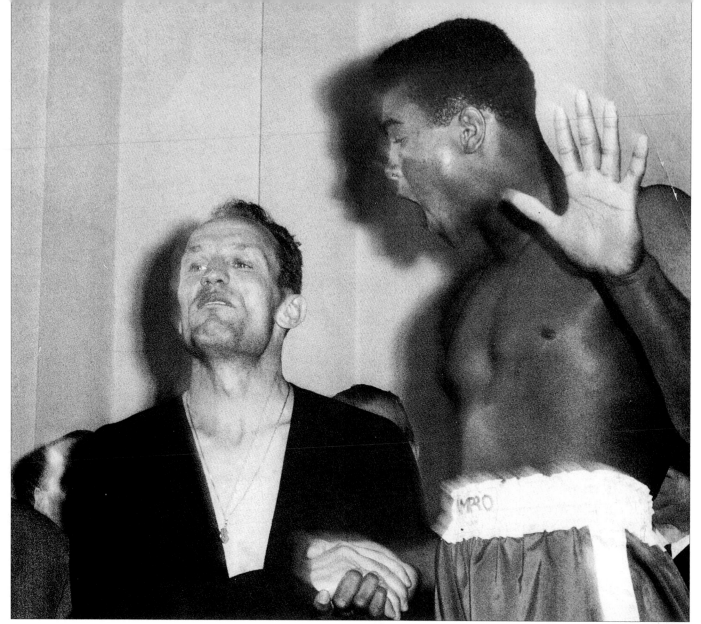

'I'll give him a good fight'

Left: Clay again holds up his hand to indicate that he will dispose of Cooper in round five, while promoter Jack Solomons and Cooper himself both look on in amusement. At the weigh-in, Clay scaled at 207lbs, while Cooper weighed in at 185½lbs - the lightest he had been for some years. Unfortunately the announcer got the weights mixed up and many onlookers went away with the impression that Clay was lighter than Cooper.

Above: At the weigh-in Clay shakes hands with Cooper before the two men were interviewed by the Press. In contrast with Clay's outrageous attire, Cooper wore a simple brown cardigan over his trunks.

Right: Clay had been roundly booed when he first arrived and he went on to deliberately incite the crowd's anger by announcing loudly, 'I'm gonna do all I said... Five rounds, man. Five... I'm gonna speak no more.' By contrast, Cooper just smiled and said, 'I'll give him a good fight.'

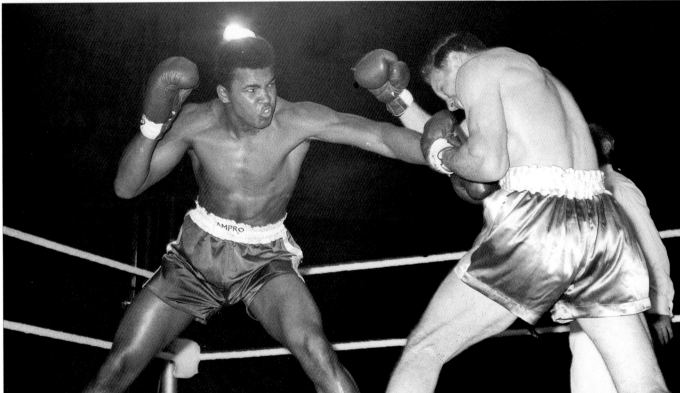

55,000 at Wembley Stadium

Opposite above: On the night of June 18, Clay paraded into the ring to a fanfare of trumpets, wearing his fancy red robe and a golden crown loaded with imitation precious jewels. A crowd of 55,000 filled open-air Wembley Stadium on the outskirts of London, to see if Clay would be able to fulfil his latest prediction.

Opposite below and above: Although Cooper attacked non-stop and did manage to land several blows, for the first three rounds and most of round four, Clay was in full control, punching Cooper pretty much at will and dancing out of the way every time he tried to retaliate.

Right: By round four, Cooper was badly bloodied and hurt. Clay had opened up a big cut above his left eye, and he seemed to keep going on courage alone. Every time he seemed ready to fall, however, Clay would step back and start preening, gazing towards the audience. William Faversham, one of his American sponsors, called for him to 'stop the funny business', but Clay took no notice.

Henry's Hammer

Above and right: While Clay was busy playing to the audience, even flirting in the direction of Elizabeth Taylor, Cooper had gathered all his strength. He takes advantage of the diversion and lets fly with his devastating left hook, which had become known as 'Henry's Hammer'. It catches Clay unawares, square on the side of his chin.

Opposite above: Clay goes over backwards into the ropes and slumps to the canvas. He did manage to struggle to his feet again, but the bell rang to signify the end of the round before the two opponents could resume fighting.

Opposite below: Before round five could begin, a slight tear in one of Clay's gloves was brought to referee Tommy Little's notice. The delay while they tried to find a replacement pair gave Clay an extra minute's rest, and as Cooper said later, '...to a fit guy, that's a lifetime.' Clay came out fighting and laid into Cooper for the next two minutes, until Little stopped the fight. Clay was the winner yet again - but he had flirted with disaster and it had been a really close call.

Opposite: A battered Cooper poses next to Clay after the fight.

Left: Back in his dressing room, Clay found Sonny Liston's manager, Jack Nilon, waiting. He had come to say that Liston wanted Clay to stay healthy; 'I've flown 3,000 miles just to tell you Liston wants you... you've talked yourself into a title fight.' Later at his London hotel, Clay responded by holding up his fingers to signify he would defeat Liston in eight.

Below: Clay, with his brother, Rudolph, faces the Press one last time before he prepares to leave London for America. 'I'm the greatest. Not only do I knock them out, I pick the round. I'm the boldest, the prettiest, the most superior, most scientific, most skilfullest fighter in the ring today. I've received more publicity than any fighter in history. I talk to reporters till their fingers are sore.'

'Liston in eight – next Champ, Cassius'

The chance to fight Liston is what Clay has been working towards ever since he turned professional. If he can take the world heavyweight title from the champion, there will be no more doubt in the sporting Press about his abilities. As he sits on his luggage at the hotel, waiting for the cars to come and take him and his entourage to the airport, he holds up eight fingers to anyone within reach.

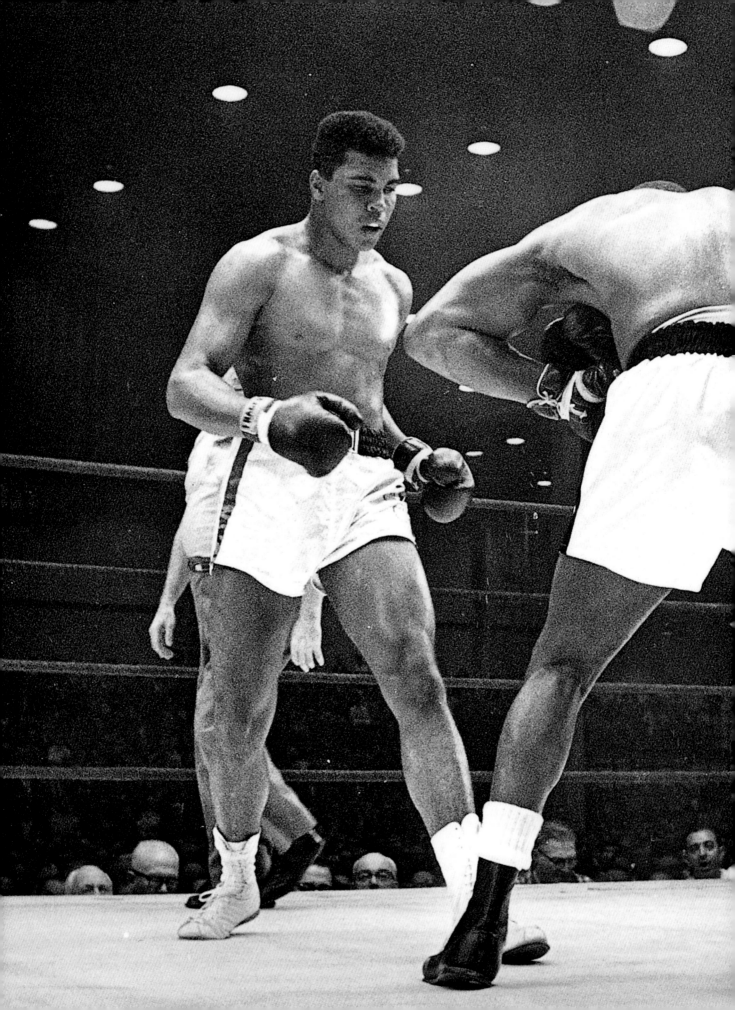

Chapter Two

'Float like a butterfly, sting like a bee'

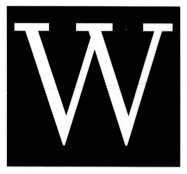hen he was the champion, Sonny Liston was thought to be unbeatable; many thought he was the best heavyweight of all time. He was not only a great fighter, he was also mean-tempered and had an intimidating reputation. He had been arrested many times, imprisoned for armed robbery and for beating up a policeman, and he was involved in organized crime. But to take the world championship, Clay had to fight him.

Clay launched a verbal campaign, goading Liston to generate publicity and get the fight off the ground. He arrived in Las Vegas before the second Liston-Patterson fight and insulted Liston at a craps game; he jumped into the ring afterwards to proclaim he was the better fighter - he even rounded up the local Press and appeared on Liston's doorstep shouting that he would 'whup Liston bad'. His tactics worked and in November 1963 a fight contract was signed, even though the Louisville Sponsoring Group didn't think he was ready to face Liston. The consensus was that Clay would lose, since he was still regarded as an unknown novice of limited talent, while Liston was a polished professional with a really powerful punch. Critics said Clay's style was all wrong: he carried his hands too low; he leant away from a punch; he danced around to avoid fighting; he couldn't punch; he fought like a bantamweight. Despite this, Clay seemed to have every confidence in himself. He studied Liston's style, trained hard and frequently announced that Liston didn't have a hope. He later admitted that part of his plan was to get Liston so angry that he'd forget all his boxing technique and just try to kill his tormentor.

As the publicity for the event was building, another storm broke. For some time there had been rumours that Clay was associating with the Nation of Islam, otherwise known as the 'Black Muslims'. Eighteen days before the Liston fight Clay's father, Cassius Senior, gave an interview to the *Miami Herald* in which he said that Clay had become a Muslim and intended to change his name after the contest. The Nation of Islam was highly unpopular and regarded as a serious threat in America, particularly in the Southern states. At this time its beliefs were very different to those of orthodox Muslims: among other things, members rejected the concepts of Heaven and Hell, which are central to traditional Islamic thought, and believed that white people were a race of devils, genetically engineered to destroy black people. They preached black pride and were against any kind of integration, instead wanting their own independent territory to achieve complete separation. Their message was a powerful one to young blacks in the early sixties, who had spent their lives as an underclass, banned from living in some areas and eating in certain restaurants and constantly treated

unjustly. One of their most prominent members was Malcolm X, who was a charismatic speaker and knew how to manipulate the media. Clay and he had become close, and he had come to Miami during the build-up for the fight to support Clay. Because of Liston's mean reputation, the Clay-Liston bout was being promoted as the 'good guy against the bad guy', but now Clay's association with Malcolm X and the Nation of Islam made him a 'bad guy' too. It put the future of the fight in the balance - particularly since it was being held in the South. The promoter wanted Clay to announce publicly that he did not support the Muslims, which Clay refused to do. Since attention was mainly being focused on Malcolm X, he was persuaded to leave Miami until the day of the fight. The media frenzy temporarily died down, and it was agreed that the bout should go ahead.

At the weigh-in Clay put on another show, shouting, trying to attack Liston and appearing to have totally lost control. Many people genuinely thought he had gone mad with fear and might fail to appear for the fight; there were even rumours that he had been seen buying a ticket to leave town. However, as early as the first round it began to seem as if things were not so clear-cut after all. Liston had disposed of his last three opponents in the first round, but Clay danced around and Liston just couldn't catch him. By the third round, Liston was already beginning to tire, and Clay went after him, opening up cuts under both eyes. At the beginning of the fifth round Clay had a problem with his eyes, but he carried on fighting and by round six he was hitting Liston at will, while Liston couldn't touch him. The seventh round never started - Liston quit in his corner because of a shoulder injury and Clay was the new heavyweight champion of the world.

Many people could hardly believe it. Here was a youngster from nowhere who behaved in an outrageous fashion, and he had beaten the champion. Moreover, at a Press conference after his victory someone inevitably asked about the 'Black Muslims' and Clay made it clear that he was a member of the Nation of Islam. Not long afterwards, he changed his name. The Muslims had taught him that most black people had names inherited from their ancestors, who had been called after their masters when they were slaves. Cassius Marcellus Clay had been a white man from Kentucky who had owned Clay's great-grandfather. Clay had been proud of his name, but now it was identified with slavery. At first he began signing autographs 'Cassius X Clay', with the X standing for his lost African identity, but in a radio broadcast on the night of March 6, 1964, Elijah Muhammad, leader of the Nation of Islam, re-named him Muhammad Ali. It all seemed rather frivolous, and at first both the media and the boxing authorities responded with anger and resentment and refused to use his new name.

The Muslims were now becoming increasingly influential in Ali's professional and personal life. Malcolm X soon left the Nation of Islam and Elijah Muhammad sent one of his sons, Herbert

Muhammad, to guide Ali. At the time, Herbert was a professional photographer and he introduced Ali to a model he knew, Sonji Roi. Sonji was very beautiful and sensual, and Ali soon asked her to marry him. Even though Herbert had introduced them he advised Ali against going ahead - Sonji was streetwise and worked in a cocktail bar, which didn't sit well with the modesty and chastity expected from Muslim women. But Ali was madly in love, and Sonji genuinely cared for him. Unfortunately the marriage didn't last long; Sonji questioned many of the beliefs of the Nation of Islam and resented the control it tried to exert over both her and Ali. Soon there were moves to come between them and by the beginning of 1966 they were divorced.

Meanwhile, Ali was preparing for the rematch against Liston, which was set for November 1964. Unfortunately, three days before the scheduled date Ali suffered a hernia and was rushed to hospital for an emergency operation. The fight had to be postponed for six months, during which Ali continued to mature as a fighter. Liston, who had been in great shape in November, had to start training all over again for May, which was damaging both physically and psychologically. Despite the previous result, Liston was still favourite – people thought the first fight had been fixed, or that Liston had genuinely injured his shoulder, or that he simply hadn't taken Ali seriously enough to train properly. In the event, the rematch was so short that some people missed it entirely - but it was still controversial. Within the first few minutes of the opening round, Ali landed a straight right that caught Liston off balance and sent him down. Instead of retiring to a neutral corner, Ali stood over Liston shaking his fist and screaming at him to get up and fight. The referee lost control and failed to count Liston out, but according to the knockdown timer he spent 17 seconds on the canvas and was therefore deemed to be out. Ali had retained his title, but once again in circumstances of confusion and ambiguity.

Clay with his brother, Rudolph, talking with Norma Lindon and Brenda Howell in the lounge of their hotel.

Opposite: Clay takes a break during training for his fight against Sonny Liston. He recognised that Liston was a formidable foe and was determined to be in the best shape possible for the bout, but the physical preparation was only part of the story - Clay was also psyching himself up mentally to meet Liston.

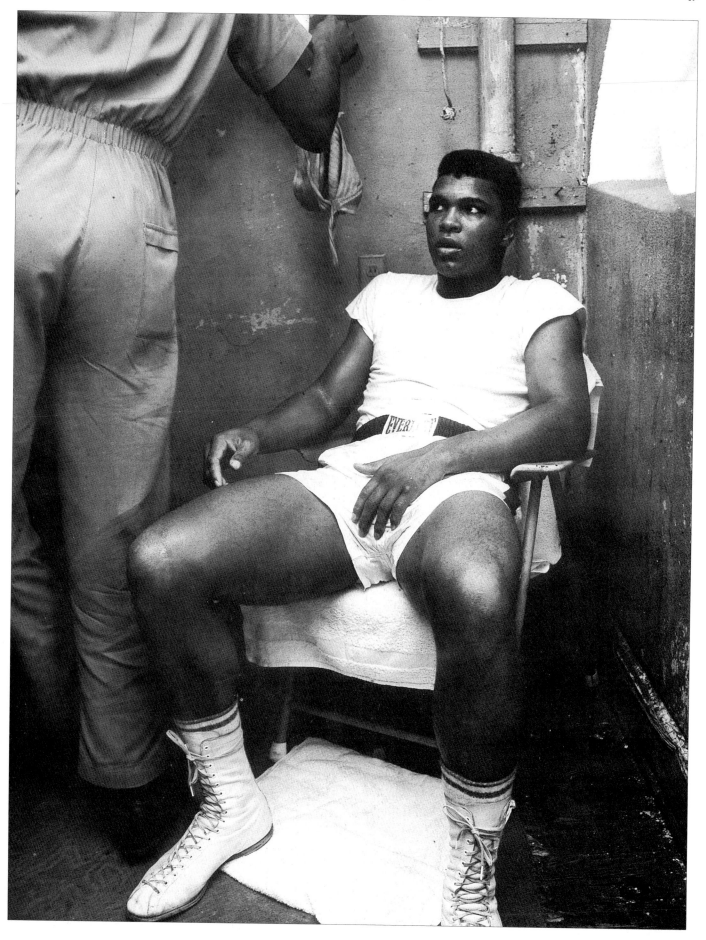

Clay poses in Miami's Fifth Street Gym for
photographers. The Clay-Liston fight was to be held in
Miami, so Clay was on home ground to train since
this was where Angelo Dundee was based. It was
Dundee who encouraged him to be open with
journalists, telling him, 'Open up to them, work with
them. They can help.' Some editors felt Liston would
destroy Clay so quickly that it was not worth sending
their main boxing writer, so they sent feature writers
instead. They were in their element, because there was
so much happening before the fight - ugly rumours,
the verbal battle between the two opponents and then
the uproar about the Nation of Islam.

'The Mouth' mouths off

Right: During the pre-fight build-up, Clay was constantly shouting about how great he was and what he was planning to do to Liston. Liston responded, 'My only worry is how I'll get my fist outta his big mouth once I get him in the ring. It's gonna go so far down his throat, it'll take a week for me to pull it out again.'

Below: Just one week to go before the fight, and Clay does some ring work with one of his sparring partners.

Opposite: Clay's training sessions were open to the public, who paid a small fee to come in and watch. They got more than just sparring, as Clay was always ready to put on a show. In these early days much of the crowd consisted of journalists and photographers who had come to cover the fight, but there was also a fair sprinkling of boxing fans - as well as members of the Nation of Islam.

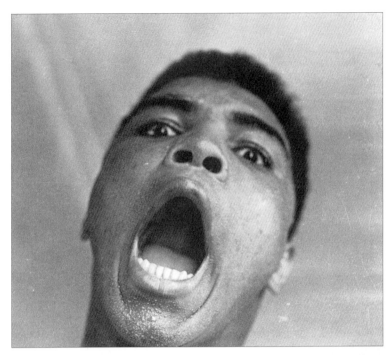

Twist and Shout

At the same time as Clay was preparing to meet Liston, The Beatles were in Miami to make a second appearance on *The Ed Sullivan Show*. Harold Conrad, who was coordinating the Clay-Liston fight promotion, arranged for them to visit Clay in the gym - along with a few journalists and photographers. Although he knew they were a group from England Clay was not a fan, but The Beatles, on their first visit to the US, were taking the country by storm so the resulting publicity was good for both sides. While they were clowning around in the ring Clay declared that he was still the greatest, but that The Beatles were the prettiest. The musicians and the boxer then began to discuss amongst themselves the money they were making. Clay was impressed. 'You're not as stupid as you look,' he commented. 'No, but you are,' came back Lennon, quick as a flash. Luckily he was smiling and Clay saw the joke.

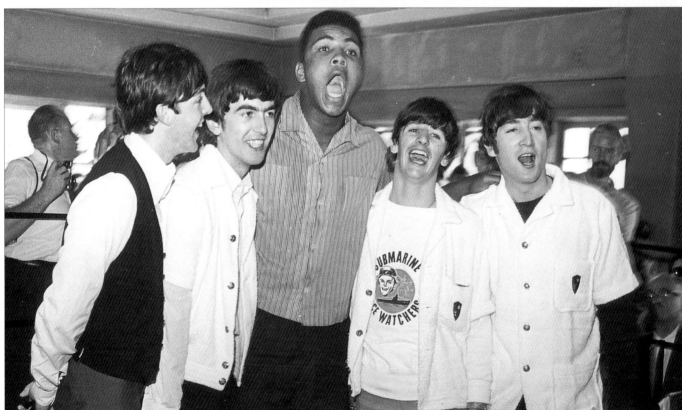

Opposite above: Clay messes about with The Beatles in the Fifth Street Gym.

Opposite below: Clay in his apartment, posing with his belt just before the Liston fight. Behind him, the sign saying 'Allah is the Greatest' is an indication that he is already a Muslim.

Right: During the pre-fight physical, Clay holds up eight fingers to predict that he will beat Liston in the eighth round.

Below: Clay is restrained from attacking Liston at the weigh-in. He put on a great show of fear and hysteria, convincing Liston that he was about to face a madman, but the whole thing was carefully planned. Although the Miami Boxing Commission physician was of the opinion that Clay was 'emotionally unbalanced, scared to death and liable to crack up before he enters the ring', his personal physician, Ferdie Pacheco, commented, 'Cassius is in complete control of himself. He knows exactly what he's doing. It's going to be a very interesting evening.'

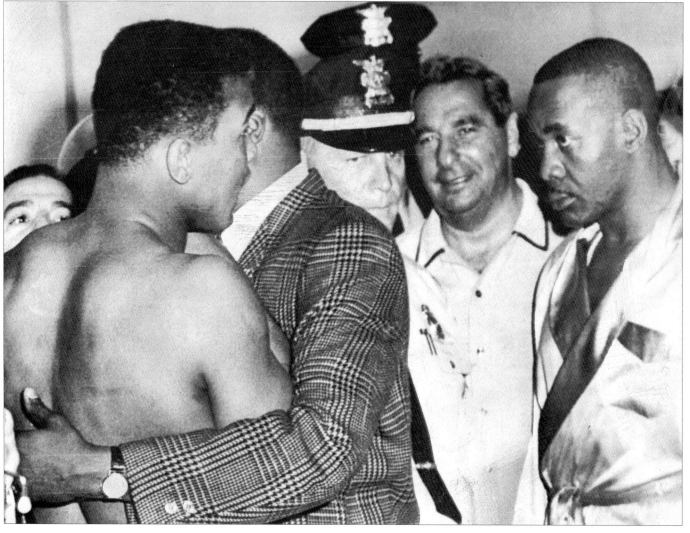

Right: Clay in action against Liston on the night of February 25, 1964. Right from the start the up-and-coming champion danced and ducked and moved so swiftly out of range, that Liston found it very difficult to land any punches.

Below: Liston was a powerful and experienced fighter and few people thought Clay had any chance against him, but part of his ability was in intimidating his opponent. Later Clay said he had been scared as the referee gave them instructions, knowing how hard Liston could hit, but he quickly regained his confidence after they began to fight.

Opposite above: Liston had a jab like a battering ram, as other fighters before Clay had discovered to their cost.

Opposite below: Clay goes on the offensive. By the third round Liston was beginning to get tired and frustrated and Clay went after him. During round four he coasted, conserving his energy, but near the end his eyes began burning. There are people who believe that Liston's corner put some sort of substance on his gloves, which would get into Clay's eyes and blind him long enough for Liston to knock him out. Later theories are that either the coagulant on Liston's cuts or the liniment on his shoulder had got onto Clay's gloves, and when he brushed them against his forehead the substance had trickled down with the perspiration into his eyes. However the problem was caused, Clay couldn't see and he wanted to stop the fight, but Dundee saved the day by washing out his eyes and pushing him out for round five, saying, 'This is the big one, daddy. Stay away from him. Run!'

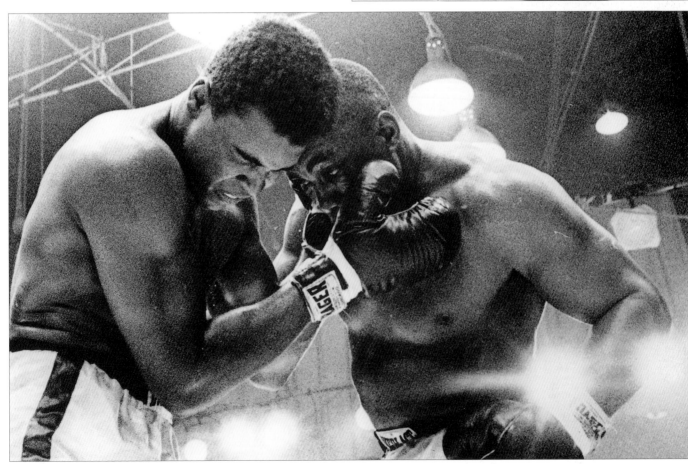

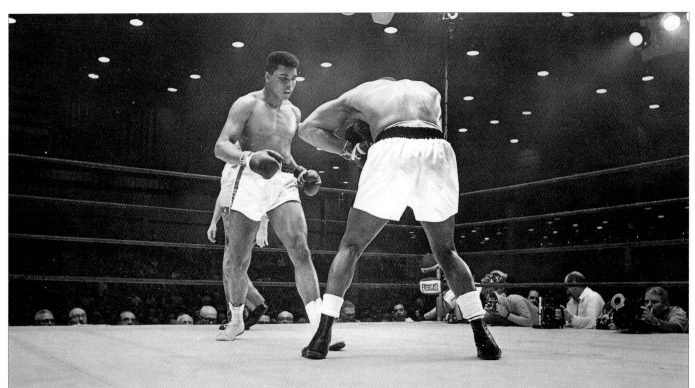

King of the world

Opposite above: As instructed, Clay kept his distance from Liston during round five, until his eyes began to clear. He still kept Liston under control, touching him when he got too close to break his concentration.

Opposite below: Midway through the fifth, Clay regained his sight and the two fighters were on even terms again.

Above: By round six Clay was in full control again, hitting Liston at will but not allowing him in close enough to retaliate. Liston could sense that the title was slipping from his grasp.

Right: When the bell rang for the start of the seventh round, Liston failed to answer. He was complaining of a sore shoulder and quit in his corner, the first heavyweight champion to do so since Jess Willard in 1919, when he fought Jack Dempsey. The new heavyweight champion of the world threw himself into the arms of one of his seconds, shouting, 'I am the greatest! I'm king of the world! I am the king!'

It was no match

Right and below: Clay's seconds are jubilant as he rushes round the ring, shouting to reporters. Journalist Howard Cosell climbed into the ring to interview him, and Clay told him, 'I'm too fast. He was scared. I knew I had him in the first round. I shook up the world! I can't be beat! I am the greatest! It was no match. I want the world to know, I'm so great that Sonny Liston was not even a match. I don't have a mark on my face. I shook up the world.'

Opposite above: Clay looks out over the crowd after his win. The venue was half empty because of a combination of factors, including the low expectation that Clay would win, high ticket prices, and the weeks of rumours about Clay being a member of the Nation of Islam.

Opposite below: A dejected Liston in his corner after his defeat. Afterwards he was taken to hospital for x-rays and for his cuts to be stitched, as his face was damaged and swollen. There he turned to his manager and said, 'That wasn't the guy I was supposed to fight. That guy could hit.'

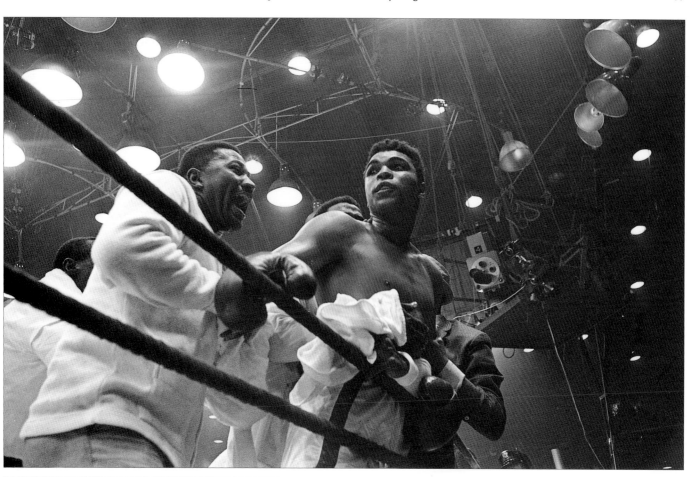

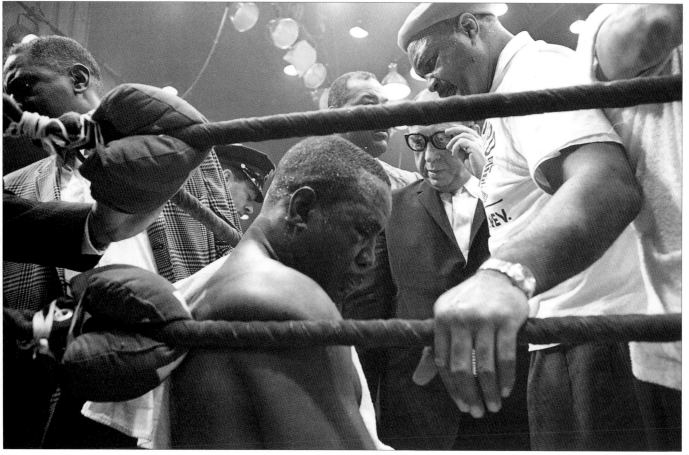

World Champion

Right: Clay leaves the ring, heading for his dressing room where he demanded that reporters acknowledged that he was the greatest.

Below: Drew Brown, who was also known as Bundini, stands to the left of Clay crying with joy at his victory. Bundini was Clay's court jester, and also provided him with constant support and encouragement. He later told reporters that he bonded with Clay before a fight to such an extent that he felt every blow.

Opposite above: Clay's parents, Odessa and Cassius Snr, were there to see their son win. His father had recently been interviewed by Pat Putnam of the *Herald*, and had told the paper about the threats to kill him that he claimed had been made by members of the Nation of Islam. He said he had accused the Nation of taking his son's money.

Opposite below: Clay hugs a fan. He was always accessible to whoever wanted to meet him and was happy to spend a great deal of time with those less fortunate than himself.

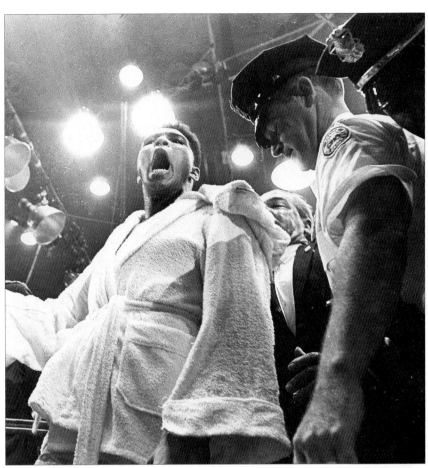

The birth of Muhammad Ali

After the fight with Liston, the new champ finally confirmed to reporters that he was a member of the Nation of Islam and a few weeks later he announced that he was now to be known as Muhammad Ali, a name he had been given by Elijah Muhammad, leader of the Nation. For a long time the Press refused to use his new name, as the Nation stood for some rather questionable things and was widely regarded as being a bit sinister. Meanwhile the movement had increasing influence on Ali, and Elijah Muhammad sent his son, Herbert, to look after Ali's interests in the world of boxing.

...the eighth wonder of the world

Left: On a visit to Egypt in June 1964, some three months after surprising the world by winning the heavyweight championship, Ali visits some of the other wonders of the world, including the Sphinx and the pyramids. Ali was under attack in America because of his membership of the Nation of Islam so the trip - which lasted a month and began with visits to Africa and Nigeria - was arranged to get him out of the country for a while, until things had settled down.

Below: Ali prays at the Hussein Mosque in Cairo.

Opposite: The famous slogan, 'Float like a butterfly, sting like a bee' was apparently invented by Bundini and it was one of the things he and Ali shouted at the weigh-in for the first Liston fight. The phrase caught the public imagination and became synonymous with Ali. Bundini later had it printed on the back of T-shirts, one of which he is wearing here for a training session in the Fifth Street Gym in Miami.

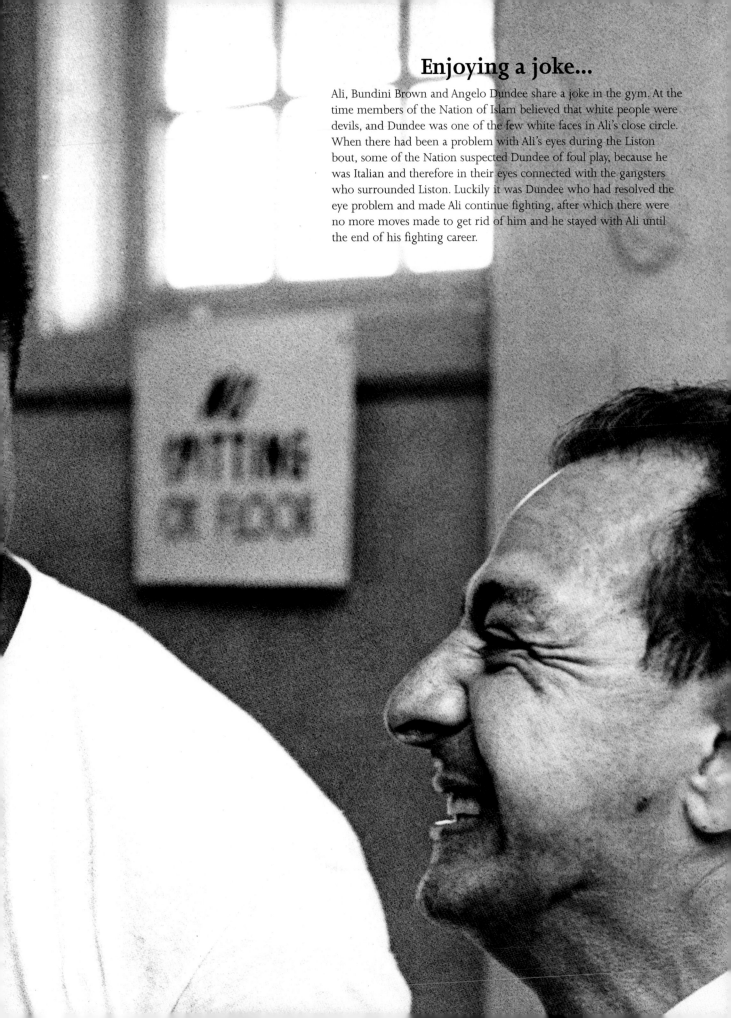

Enjoying a joke...

Ali, Bundini Brown and Angelo Dundee share a joke in the gym. At the time members of the Nation of Islam believed that white people were devils, and Dundee was one of the few white faces in Ali's close circle. When there had been a problem with Ali's eyes during the Liston bout, some of the Nation suspected Dundee of foul play, because he was Italian and therefore in their eyes connected with the gangsters who surrounded Liston. Luckily it was Dundee who had resolved the eye problem and made Ali continue fighting, after which there were no more moves made to get rid of him and he stayed with Ali until the end of his fighting career.

Liston rematch setback

Ali takes a few days off in Miami and visits the Sea World aquarium. After making a mock challenge to one of the dolphins, he said, 'It looks like I finally met someone with a bigger mouth than me.'

Opposite: A rematch against Liston has already been scheduled for November 16, 1964, so Ali was keeping up his training. In the event, Ali was rushed to hospital three days before the fight, suffering from a hernia. One of the surgeons who operated on him later said, 'It was such a marvellously developed stomach, I hated to slice it up.' Medical opinion was that the defect had been present since birth and could have caused a problem at any time, but Liston thought otherwise. 'If he'd stop all that hollering, he wouldn't have a hernia,' he was reported as saying in *Life*.

The fight was rescheduled for May 25 the following year; the setback was more of a problem for Liston than Ali, as he was that much older and found it more difficult to retain his fitness, while Ali was still maturing as a fighter.

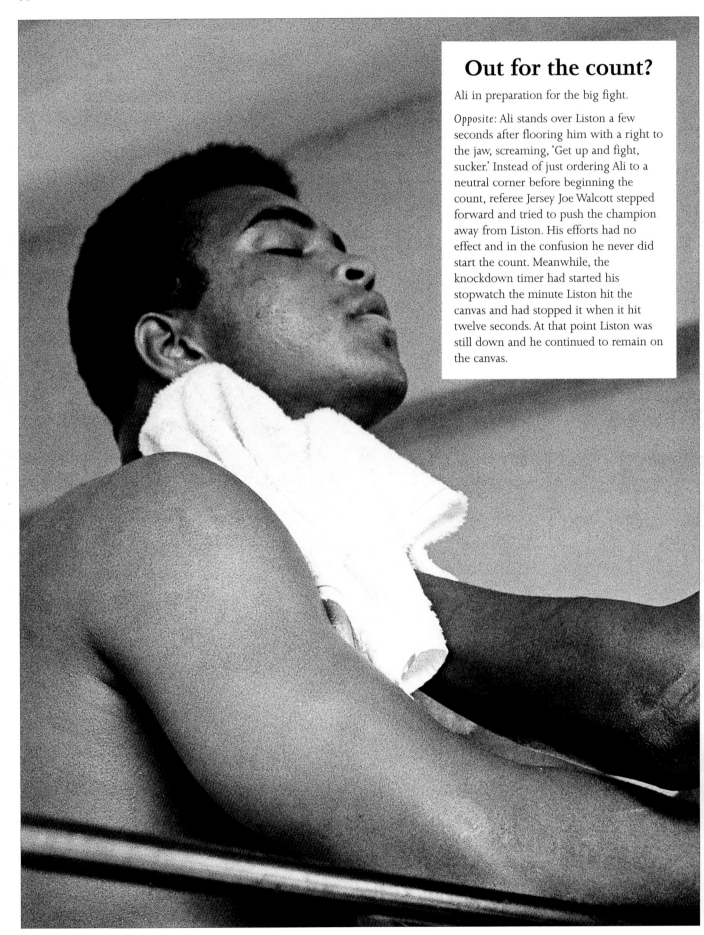

Out for the count?

Ali in preparation for the big fight.

Opposite: Ali stands over Liston a few seconds after flooring him with a right to the jaw, screaming, 'Get up and fight, sucker.' Instead of just ordering Ali to a neutral corner before beginning the count, referee Jersey Joe Walcott stepped forward and tried to push the champion away from Liston. His efforts had no effect and in the confusion he never did start the count. Meanwhile, the knockdown timer had started his stopwatch the minute Liston hit the canvas and had stopped it when it hit twelve seconds. At that point Liston was still down and he continued to remain on the canvas.

'I got excited'

Ali later said, 'It was a good punch, but I didn't think I hit him so hard that he couldn't have gotten up. Once he went down, I got excited; I forgot about the rules... people said maybe the first fight was fixed. So the second time I wanted to whup him bad. I didn't want him making excuses, or quitting. I wanted him to get up, so I could show everyone how great I was.'

Liston later said that he didn't get up because in doing so he would have been exposed to a great shot. Since he thought Ali was an unpredictable madman and the referee had lost control, he wasn't about to take the risk.

Opposite above: After Ali was safely in a neutral corner, Liston got to his feet, Walcott wiped his gloves and the fight resumed. However, after being told by Nat Fleischer, influential editor of *Ring* magazine - who was sitting next to the knockout timer - that Liston had been on the canvas for more than ten seconds, Walcott runs forward to stop the fight.

Opposite below: Former champion Floyd Patterson congratulates Ali on his victory.

Heading for divorce

Right and below: Ali's first wife, Sonji Roi, whom he married in August 1964 and divorced not long after the second Liston fight. He and Sonji were very much in love, but the Nation of Islam came between them. She had agreed to observe dietary laws, attended meetings and services, and didn't drink or smoke, but she refused to stop wearing make-up and dress in modest, floor-length clothing. She could also see that some of the stranger ideas - which were later dropped as the Nation moved towards orthodox Islam - didn't make any sense, and had no hesitation in pointing it out. Eventually he had to chose between her and his religion, and the Nation won. Despite this Ali was heartbroken, saying later that he sat in his room, smelling her perfume and going crazy staring at the walls. In time he started seeing other women and later had a reputation as a world-class womanizer, but while married to Sonji he had been a faithful husband.

Opposite: Ali enjoys supper in a restaurant. Despite the wine glasses, he had never drunk alcohol and after he became a Muslim he also stopped eating pork.

Fighter of the Year

Opposite: Despite the controversy over his wins against Liston, Ali was presented with the Edward J Neil trophy as the Fighter of the Year of 1965, at the annual awards dinner of the Boxing Writers' Association of New York. The trophy had first been presented to Jack Dempsey in 1938.

There was still a great deal of criticism in the Press - and not only about Ali's religious views. Many sporting pundits were still reluctant to accept that he could fight. Even former champion Joe Louis announced that Ali couldn't punch and that he couldn't take a punch. 'He's lucky there are no good fighters around... I would have whipped him.' Ali's response was swift. 'Joe Louis beat me... would I just quit dancing that night and stand there and let him hit me?'

Opposite: Ali arrives in London from Sweden, on his way to fight an exhibition match in Paisley, Scotland. The champ was strangely subdued, announcing that he had given up predicting and name-calling, and that he needed some rest.

Floyd Patterson falls during his fight with Ali on November 22, 1965. He soon recovers, but Ali ducks under his jab.

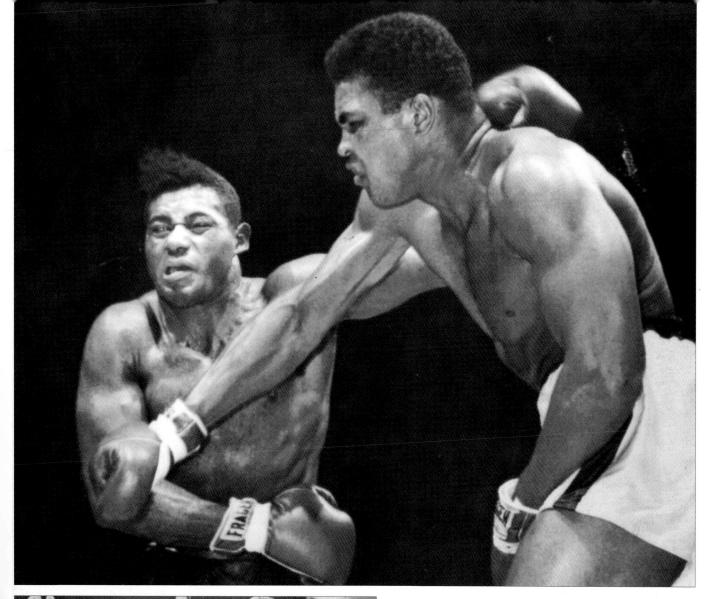

'Sickening Spectacle in a ring'

Opposite: Ali goes after Patterson in the ring. The pre-fight build-up had turned ugly when Patterson said he was going to remove the 'Black Muslim' influence from boxing and 'reclaim the title for America'. He saw himself as a righteous Christian, saving the world of boxing from infidel usurpers.

Above: During the fight, Patterson was hopelessly outclassed and Ali danced rings around him, hitting him at will but stepping back each time and refusing to knock him out.

Left: Referee Harry Krause springs forward to take Ali back to a neutral corner, while Patterson clambers to his feet again. Ali prolonged the fight into round twelve, at which point Krause finally stopped it. The following days brought Ali another round of censure in the Press, with *Life* magazine headlining its story 'Sickening Spectacle in a Ring'. Ali said, 'If I knock him out fast, you'd say it was fixed. If I knock him out slow, I'm a brute. I'm wrong if I do. I'm wrong if I don't.'

Chapter Three

'I ain't got no quarrel with them Vietcong'

t soon became apparent even to his detractors that Ali took his commitment to the Nation of Islam seriously. He attended the temple regularly for meetings, studied all the publications and often made statements about his religion and what it stood for. He spoke with Elijah Muhammad regularly and appeared at rallies, often getting up to speak. As a well-known sportsman people wanted to hear what he had to say, so his prominence helped to spread knowledge of the Nation of Islam around the world and attracted numerous converts. However, many people took exception to his pronouncements; they felt boxing should be above religion and that the heavyweight champion of the world should not be using his position as a soapbox for his beliefs. One of the main objections to the Nation of Islam was their wish for segregation and the branding of white people as devils - although Ali himself was obviously not anti-white. Angelo Dundee, his trainer, was white, and also his personal physician, Ferdie Pacheco, as well as most of the Press and those who ran boxing, and Ali got on very well with all of them. After Elijah Muhammad died in 1975, his son Wallace took over as leader of the Nation. He had learned the true nature of Islam from his studies, and he guided the movement back to follow the teaching of the Qur'an much more closely. As well as being encouraged to regard white people as devils, members had once been taught that a wheel-shaped Mother of Planes half a mile wide, which was built and manned by black men, circled the world at night. A few days before Allah's chosen day of retribution, the Mother of Planes would release Arabic language pamphlets telling the righteous where to go to be saved, and then 1,500 planes would drop explosives to destroy all unbelievers. Beliefs such as this - which had not come from the Qur'an - were dropped and the colour of someone's skin was no longer an issue. Herbert Muhammad later explained the earlier beliefs by saying that his father had sought to give black people a sense of importance and destroy their feelings of inferiority, to enable them to have self-respect. Once this had been accomplished, it was time to move on.

But a bigger quarrel connected to Ali's religion was brewing. The Vietnam war was still raging and all across America, young men were being called up to join the military. Ali had originally been classified in 1962 as 1-A, and therefore eligible for the draft, but the results of two Army mental aptitude tests in 1964 had only given him an IQ score of 78%, which was below the passing grade for the draft. He had subsequently been reclassified as 1-Y 'not qualified under current standards for service in the armed forces'. Ali was very embarrassed about the results, but he had not done at all well at high school and was particularly poor at maths. Much later, two of his children were diagnosed as being dyslexic, so it is possible he was too. By 1966, however, the war in Vietnam was escalating so much that the military lowered their mental aptitude standards and Ali was suddenly reclassified as 1-A. The Press spotted an opportunity to create a story and telephoned his home repeatedly immediately after the news broke, asking Ali for his comments on the reclassification, on the war and about how he felt about having to go to Vietnam, until he snapped, 'Man, I ain't got no quarrel with them Vietcong.'

His comment made headline news around America the next day and the consequences were immediate. Now, to his enemies, he was not only a member of a 'race-hate cult', he was also an unpatriotic draft-dodger. His next fight, against World Boxing Association champion Ernie Terrell, was already scheduled for March in Chicago, but calls were made for it to be banned. Ali appeared before the State Commission and told them, 'I'm here because certain people would be hurt financially over what I said, and you people were put on the spot before your governor and other authorities.' When pressed about whether he was apologizing for his comment, he finally stated, 'I don't have to apologize; I'm not in court.' Without waiting for the Commission to act, the Illinois Attorney General ruled that the bout violated state law, for failing to comply with three extremely obscure rules that had never before been enforced. The promoters tried to move the bout to various other US cities, but political pressure was brought to bear in each so none were prepared to take the fight. Finally it was moved to Toronto in Canada, but meanwhile the potential revenue was falling so Ernie Terrell - who was being paid a percentage - saw his financial incentive falling away and he decided to drop out. Ali finally ended up fighting the Canadian heavyweight champion, George Chuvalo, who was held to be impossible to knock out, but who lacked the skills to cope with Ali's speed. The bout went the full fifteen rounds, but the challenger won only one and because of all the controversy the event lost a lot of money for the promoters.

It was also evident that Ali was now so unpopular in America that it would be difficult to make serious money staging his fights anywhere in the country. Bouts for the world heavyweight title had been fought almost exclusively in America for over fifty years, but now Ali began to go abroad to defend his title, starting with Henry Cooper in England. Ali-Cooper was the biggest fight that had ever been staged in England, and the publicity was enormous. Cooper was the British heavyweight champion, fighting for the world championship on home ground, and Ali was already a well-known figure even outside boxing circles. Even though Cooper was 32 years old and Ali was only 24 and in his prime, many thought that Cooper had a real chance of winning because in their last encounter he had almost knocked Ali out. The fight lasted for six rounds and was really close on points, but then Ali cut Cooper over his left eye really badly and blood gushed out over the canvas. Ali knew the fight was over and told the referee he should stop it; 30 seconds later he did.

Meanwhile Ali was also still fighting the draft, partly on grounds of the financial hardship his parents would suffer without his earnings, but mainly by claiming conscientious-objector status. To be granted this, he had to appear at a special hearing and convince the presiding officer that his objection to military service was sincere, that it was based on religious training and belief, and that he was opposed to all war. The army had offered to put him into Special Services, which meant that he would spend his time boxing exhibitions for the entertainment of the troops and never have to pick up a weapon. However, Ali stated that according to his religious beliefs and the Holy Qur'an, Muslims should not participate in wars in any way on the side of non-believers. Since America was a Christian country and not a Muslim country, he could not go to Vietnam in any capacity. The presiding officer, Lawrence Grauman - a former Kentucky State Circuit Court Judge - surprised everyone by ruling that Ali's religious beliefs were sincere and recommending that his claim to conscientious-objector status should be sustained. Despite this, the Department of Justice wrote to the Appeal Board opposing the judge's decision. Following a detailed FBI investigation of Ali, they believed that his objection to war was based on political and racial factors rather than genuine religious grounds, and that he was only opposed to certain types of war. Ali's claim was subsequently denied, so his 1-A classification remained in place.

Fit for service

Right: Ali is given his pre-fight medical examination before defending his championship against George Chuvalo. Chuvalo stands between Ali and the doctor, watching closely. Both fighters are proclaimed physically fit for the bout, which is scheduled for March 29, 1965. The previous month Ali had been reclassified as fit for draft and had made his famous remark about the Vietcong, which had caused an uproar. His arranged bout against Ernie Terrell in Chicago fell apart so the fight was moved to Toronto, and Chuvalo, the Canadian heavyweight champion, was his new opponent. He beat Chuvalo, but it was a hard fight which went to round fifteen.

Below: Ali looks unhappy at a Press conference. His problems with the American military were becoming serious and he had appeared before the draft board to claim exemption on conscientious-objector status and on financial grounds.

Above: Meanwhile, the divorce had been made final and Ali's ex-wife, Sonji, was getting on with her life by launching a new career as a singer. She had recently almost had Ali put in prison over non-payment of her monthly alimony of US$1250. Sonji never took the name Ali, preferring to be known as Mrs Cassius Clay.

Right: Ali waves to his fans as he arrives in London in May 1966 to fight Henry Cooper again. The fight against Chuvalo had lost money for the promoters because of the controversy surrounding Ali, so his next three championship fights were arranged in Europe.

Opposite: Ali is met at the airport and welcomed to England by fight promoter Harry Levene, with fight manager Mickey Duff in the background.

Red-carpet treatment...

Opposite: Ali jokes with Levene and Duff at the airport. One face that is missing from Ali's entourage is Bundini, who has been exiled for pawning Ali's championship belt for US$500.

Left: Before leaving the airport, the champ gives a Press conference. Since Cooper had managed to knock Ali down during their first fight, there were great hopes that this time he might manage to win and take the title.

Below: Ali received the full red-carpet treatment in Britain, including a Rolls-Royce to take him from the airport to the Piccadilly Hotel, where he was booked into a suite.

A warm welcome

Ali arrives at his London hotel and has a smile and a wave for the
crowds of cheering fans who have come to welcome him - despite
having just arrived from Miami after a journey that had taken 24
hours. Fog over London meant his plane was diverted to Shannon,
where the champ took a nap and later enjoyed an Irish coffee with
his breakfast. Last time he came to London he was less well-known
except in sporting circles, but now his popularity has already
transcended the world of boxing.

Ali thrills the kids

Right: Ali is shepherded through the crush of fans outside his hotel by a British Bobby.

Below: Ali shakes hands with a small girl in the waiting crowd as he arrives to visit the London Free School in Tavistock Crescent, a social and educational establishment run by Notting Hill residents.

Opposite: Ali stayed in the school for half an hour, chatting and playing with the children and signing autographs for them on scraps of paper torn from a spiral-bound notepad. The visit had been arranged by one of the teachers, Michael X, who was also leader of the Racial Adjustment Action Society - the closest counterpart to the Nation of Islam in Britain. Michael X had been a friend of Malcolm X, and there were comments that he was just using Ali to promote the aims of British 'Black Muslims'. However, Mrs Rosanna Laslett, secretary of the school said, 'The children who met Muhammad Ali were thrilled. The champ obviously loves kids. He was perfectly at ease with them and talked to each one very quietly and with great understanding.'

Notting Hill

Above: When he left the London Free School, Ali's route from the door to his car was lined with 24 broad-shouldered members of the Racial Adjustment Action Society, who were acting as his bodyguard for the visit. Michael X said their presence was necessary to keep back the crowd of 300 multi-racial Notting Hill residents and prevent a stampede. As he left the building, Ali paused for a full five minutes on the top step as he silently accepted the screams, shouts of encouragement and the odd boo from the crowd.

Left: Ali's car almost disappeared beneath a mob of fans as he tried to get into it. Then he spotted a man holding up his pretty 18-month-old baby. Taking the child, the champ lifted her high in the air, kissed her and then handed her back to her delighted father.

Opposite above: Herbert Muhammad and Angelo Dundee take tea with Ali in his hotel.

Opposite below: Ali pauses to give his autograph during a stroll around London.

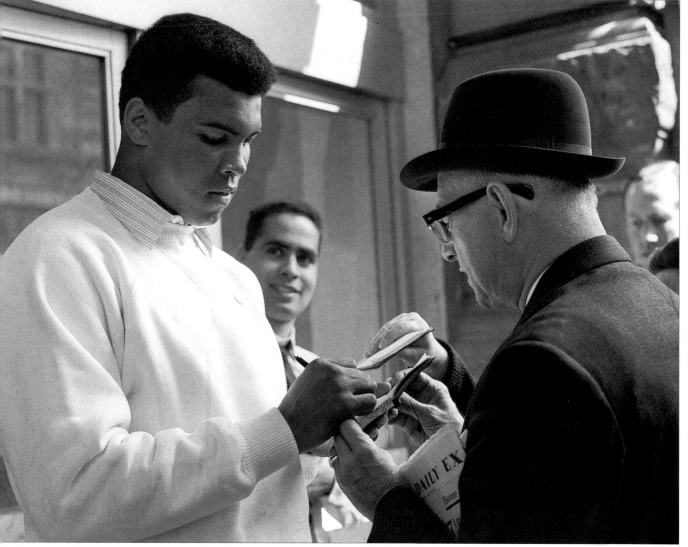

In good condition

Opposite: Ali leaves the Piccadilly Hotel on his own for a stroll round the nearby shops. Despite the controversy throughout his life he scorned most security precautions and never stopped moving freely in public. He believed that no human could keep someone from shooting him but that Allah would watch over him.

Right: Ali and Cooper exchange mock punches on meeting for a Press conference before the fight. Ali commented that Cooper had hit him with the hardest punch he had ever taken last time they met, but that he was in good condition and ready for all comers.

Below and overleaf: The two opponents fool around for the sake of the cameras. Ali was much more subdued than he had been, telling journalists that now he had been accepted as the champ, he thought the need for hollering and shouting had departed. He refused to be drawn into any predictions for the forthcoming bout, just saying that he aimed to be fast and that it was going to be a good fight.

'Only a few politicians against me'

Opposite above: Ali and Cooper compare reach, watched by promoter Harry Levene.

Opposite below: Ali returns to the hotel in his new clothes after a shopping spree at men's outfitter Cecil Gee in Piccadilly.

Right: On his way into a training session, Ali is almost mobbed by enthusiastic fans.

Below: At another Press conference, in Isow's restaurant in London's Soho on May 19, Ali shakes hands with Levene, while Dundee points out something of interest on the other side of the room. As usual, Ali is immaculately dressed - this time in a silk sports jacket with dress shirt and black bow tie.

When asked about the controversy in the United States after his comments on the Vietnam war, Ali replied, 'The mass of people like me. It is only a few politicians who are against me.'

A word from the champ

Above: Ali answers questions at the Press conference, flanked by Herbert Muhammad on the left and Dundee and Levene seated on the right. Although people in Britain hoped that Cooper had a real chance of taking the title, he was now 32 - six and a half years older than Ali - which was enough to make a big difference to his stamina in the ring. He also had an ongoing problem with cuts around the eye, because of weak tissue and prominent bones there.

There was little Press interest in England about Ali's draft problems, although at this period he was still waiting to see if his conscientious-objector status would be upheld.

Opposite: As Ali walks back to his hotel along Wardour Street after the morning Press conference, he quickly attracts a crowd of onlookers and fans. At 6'3" Ali towers over most of those around him, although he never seemed so big in isolation, because he was so perfectly proportioned.

Thumbs up!

Ali gives the thumbs up as he shows off a silver replica of a boxing ring, which was presented to him in England by the Boxing Writers' Club.

Opposite above: Ali takes a break from training, to talk to onlookers. As on his previous visit to fight Cooper, he was based at the Territorial Army gym in White City, London.

Opposite below: Working at his punch bag, Ali is surrounded by an admiring audience. He had brought his own 83lb bag with him, which had cost a fortune in excess baggage.

Ali and his sparring partner, Jimmy Ellis, take a rest on a park bench after their early morning run in Hyde Park. Despite Ali's efforts at encouragement, the corgi obviously didn't want to play ball.

A comfortable working relationship...

Dundee and Ali both have serious faces as the trainer carefully tapes the hands of the champ before a sparring session at the gym in White City. Ali's sparring partner, Jimmy Ellis, was an old friend of his from Louisville and had been brought to Miami and introduced to Dundee by Ali. They had been sparring together since before the first Cooper fight, so they had a comfortable working relationship. Ellis later said that they had both improved as fighters during this period, as they made each other work.

While watching Ali spar in London, onlooker Terry Downes said, 'I've never seen a guy roll his head away from punches like that. Fantastic!'

The fight is just over a week away now, and Cooper is also busy training on the other side of London, in the Thomas A'Beckett Gym in the Old Kent Road. His sparring partner is another American, heavyweight Jimmy Fletcher.

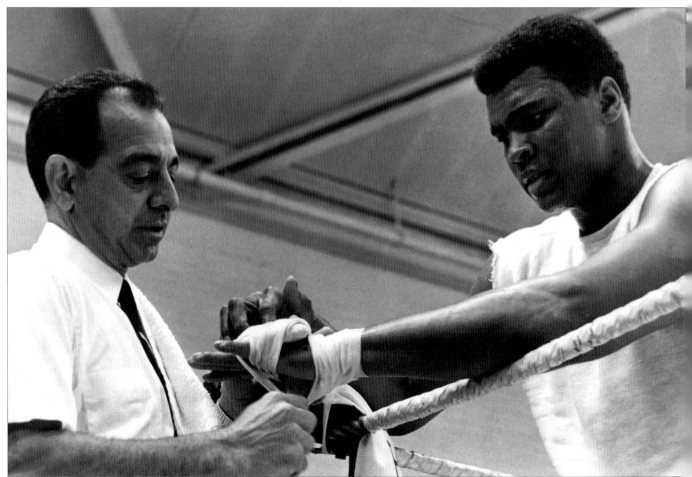

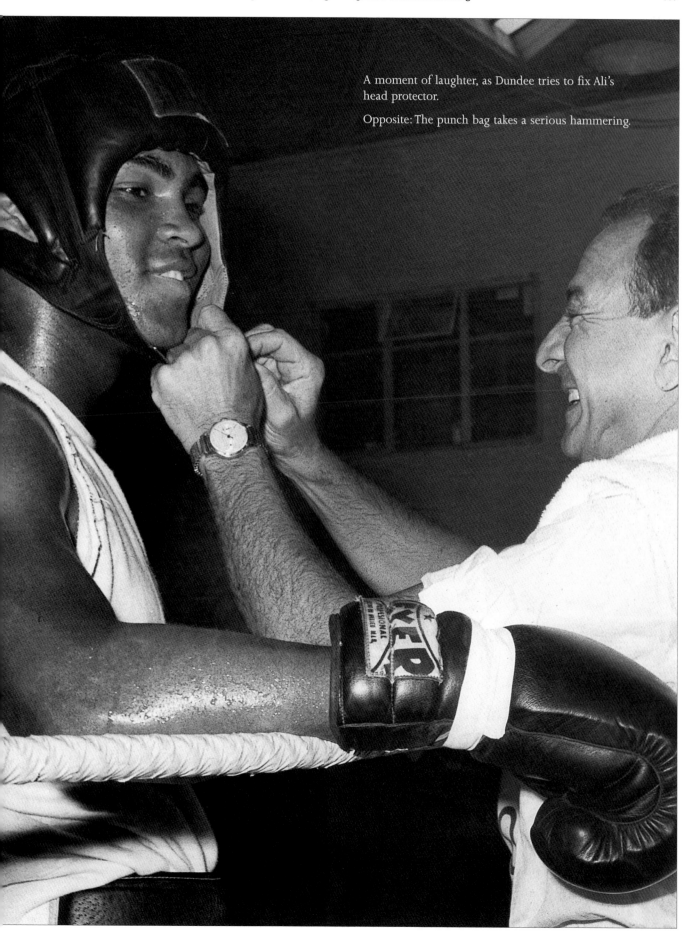

A moment of laughter, as Dundee tries to fix Ali's head protector.

Opposite: The punch bag takes a serious hammering.

... and the champ is down!

Left: Ali meets eight-month-old Maria Morin during a break from his training session. She is one female who seems more interested in the camera than the famous man holding her.

Below: Time to catch up on some news and views, as the champ takes a quick sit-down. He was fascinated to hear from a Russian journalist that boxers in the Soviet Union studied films of his fights to learn his fluid style. Ali warned, 'It's not just a question of copying. The way I box, I make it look easy. But the fella must be in condition. Got to do your roadwork, then you can hit and move and not be hit.'

Opposite above: Ali down! Not by a knockout though - he had just slipped and fallen while sparring during a training session, much to the amusement of some onlookers.

Opposite below: During sparring sessions Ali often allowed himself to be hit pretty hard, especially by his old friend Jimmy Ellis. It seemed to be part of his strategy before a fight, to sharpen his defence and build his endurance.

During one training session, Ali revealed to reporters that he had been having trouble with his hands for over a year. He had not hit the punch bag before either the Chuvalo fight or the Patterson fight the previous year. 'The hardest thing I hit for those fights was my opponents. I just had to stop punching the bag. I had a lot of pain. My hands were bleeding after every training session.' He showed the scarred knuckles that had caused the problem, but said it had now been straightened out. Dundee added, 'We've kept it a secret, but it's been a worrying time.'

Fight fever grips the West End

Above: The last session of punching the bag and sparring was on May 19 for both fighters. After this, they relied on road work and general exercise,to build speed and tune fitness. Ali spends some time skipping, watched appraisingly by his trainer, Dundee.

Left: Ali strikes a pose for photographers in his fight gear.

Right: Ali waves to onlookers as he arrives at the stage door of the Odeon, Leicester Square for the weigh-in. Fight fever had gripped the West End as the day of the fight finally arrived, and crowds thronged Leicester Square during the morning, waiting to watch the weigh-in of the two opponents. Ali had started the day with a 7 a.m. run in Hyde Park, pausing briefly to chat with Corporal Keith Marshall of the Household Cavalry, who was out for a ride on his horse Londonderry.

Cooper went for a stroll round Welling, Kent, his fight headquarters, before making the 45-minute journey into town in a dark green, chauffeur-driven Rolls-Royce. He was accompanied by his manager, Jim Wicks, and his trainer, Danny Holland.

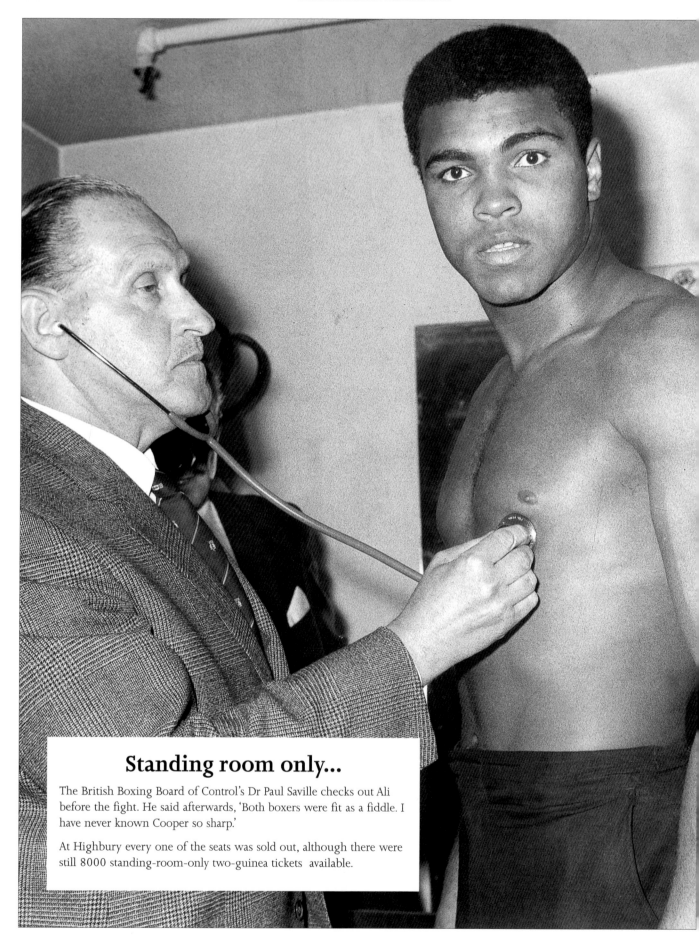

Standing room only...

The British Boxing Board of Control's Dr Paul Saville checks out Ali before the fight. He said afterwards, 'Both boxers were fit as a fiddle. I have never known Cooper so sharp.'

At Highbury every one of the seats was sold out, although there were still 8000 standing-room-only two-guinea tickets available.

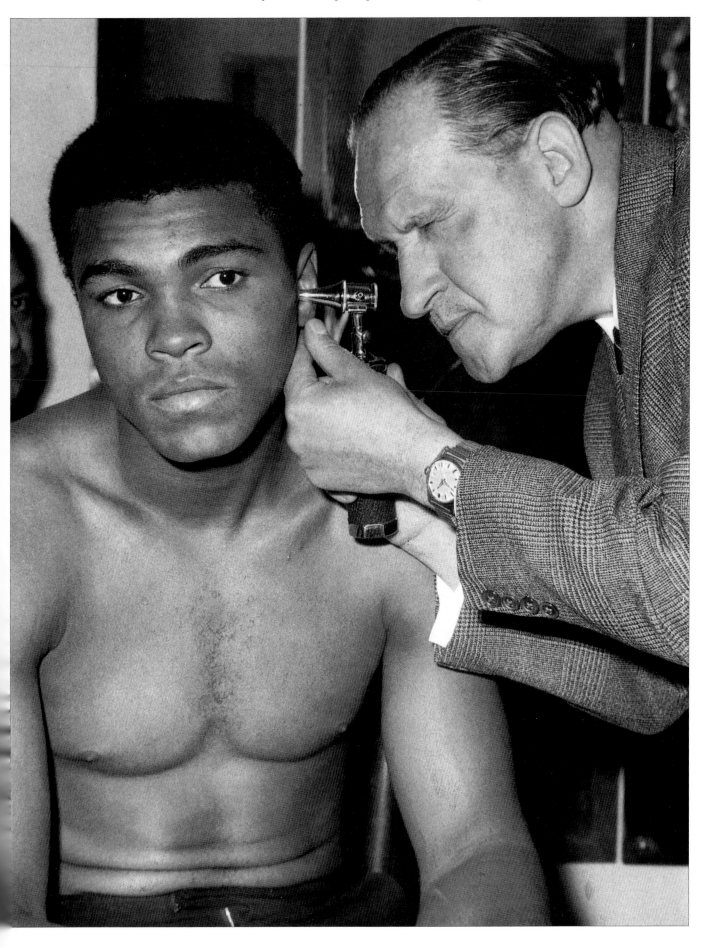

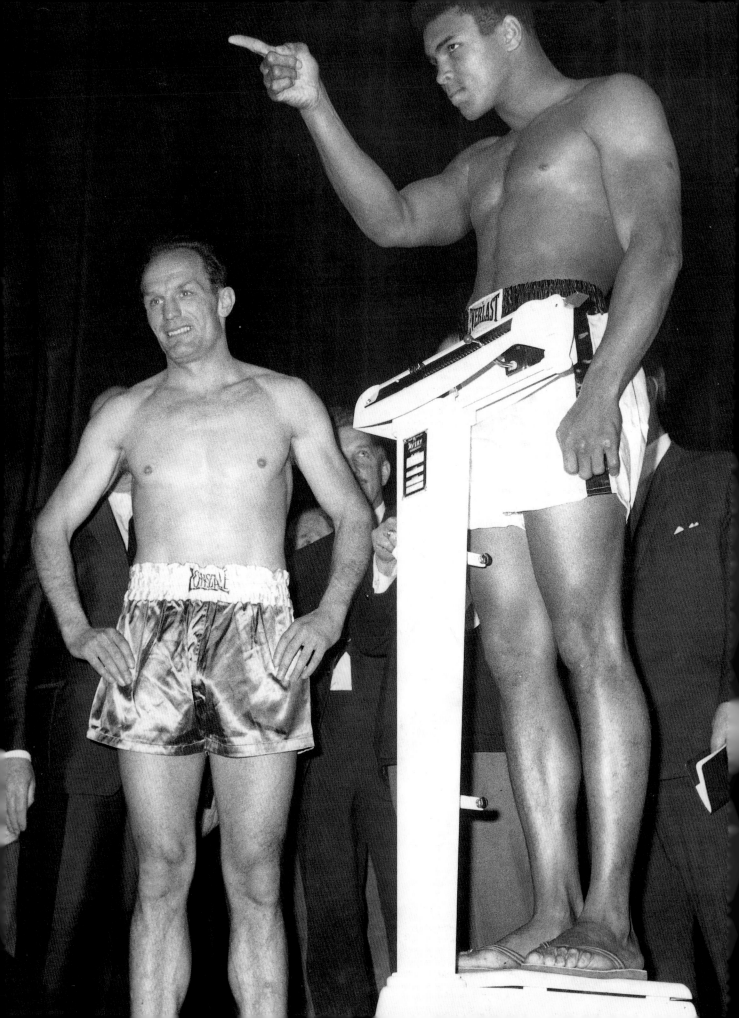

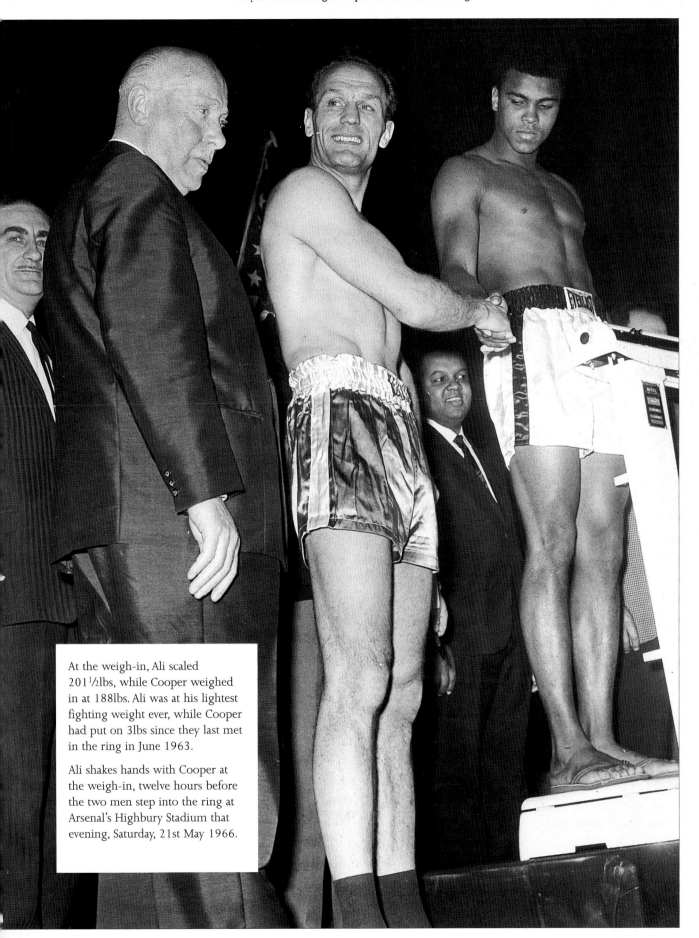

At the weigh-in, Ali scaled 201½lbs, while Cooper weighed in at 188lbs. Ali was at his lightest fighting weight ever, while Cooper had put on 3lbs since they last met in the ring in June 1963.

Ali shakes hands with Cooper at the weigh-in, twelve hours before the two men step into the ring at Arsenal's Highbury Stadium that evening, Saturday, 21st May 1966.

May the best man win...

Right: More than a thousand people watched the weigh-in and at least another thousand were locked out. Ali said, 'If Allah has willed, I will be the victor.'

Cooper retorted, 'I feel I can pull it off for the British public.'

Below: More than 45,000 people packed Highbury - the home of Arsenal Football Club - to see the fight on Saturday evening, as well as 200 members of the Press. A further 30,000 saw it live on pay television and an estimated 20 million watched in America via satelite. It had also been planned to show the bout on closed-circuit television in 20 cinemas within 70 miles of London, but it proved too difficult to get the Post Office lines at short notice. It was shown on CCTV at three London cinemas.

Opposite: Cooper began the fight ready to chase his opponent, but his age and disadvantage in height, weight and reach were against him.

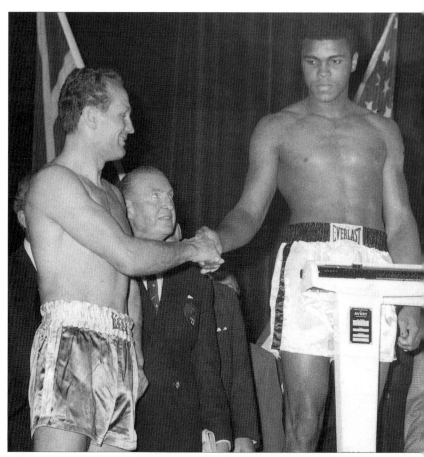

Close on points

Opposite: Cooper's pugilistic armoury was still dominated by his left hook, although in training he had tried to throw more rights than usual. Although his basic fitness was good, he had not attempted to chase his sparring partner to improve his speed. In fact Fletcher showed none of Ali's lightning evasiveness, so he may not have been the right partner to prepare Cooper for the forthcoming bout.

Above and right: Cooper's famed left hook went whistling by Ali's chin again and again. He did catch Ali in the second and third rounds with a couple of lefts and rights, and Ali said later that one punch had really hurt - although when pushed he couldn't recall in which round it had happened.

Despite his problems landing a punch, Cooper kept on coming and was only just behind on points throughout the bout.

Missed shot

Ali throws a right but misses as the British challenger ducks during the fourth round.

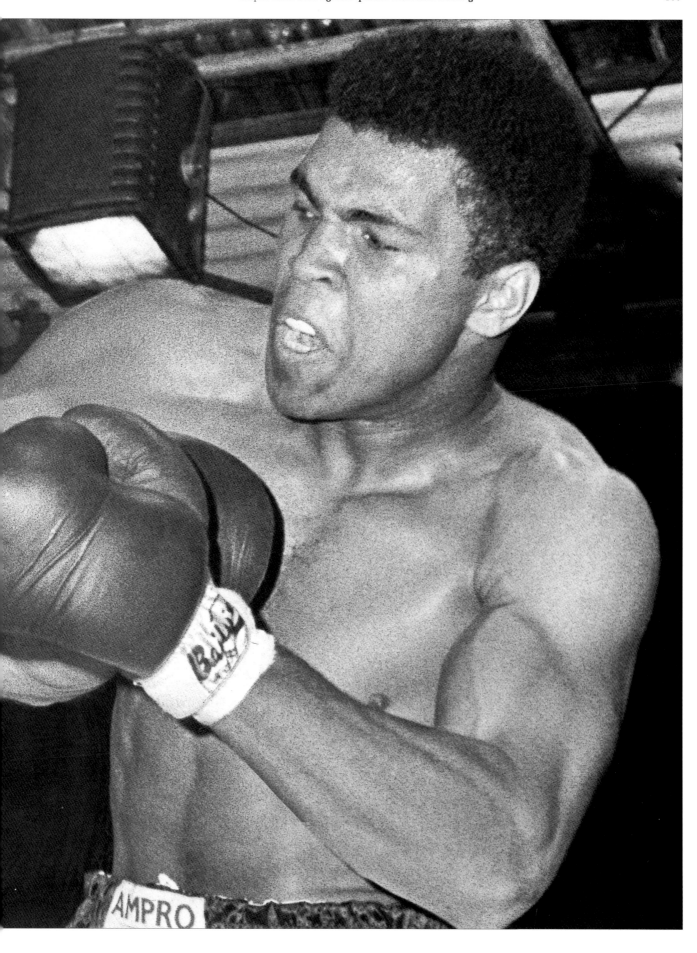

Cooper cut

However hard Cooper fought, there was a feeling of
inevitability about the outcome from the moment Ali
smashed home two lightning lefts to the face at the
end of the fourth round. In the sixth round he opened
up a cut above Cooper's left eye, which began bleeding
profusely. Cooper later said that he thought the cut had
been caused by a clash of heads, but films of the fight
clearly show a fast left and right to skin already worn
thin by 13 years in the professional ring.

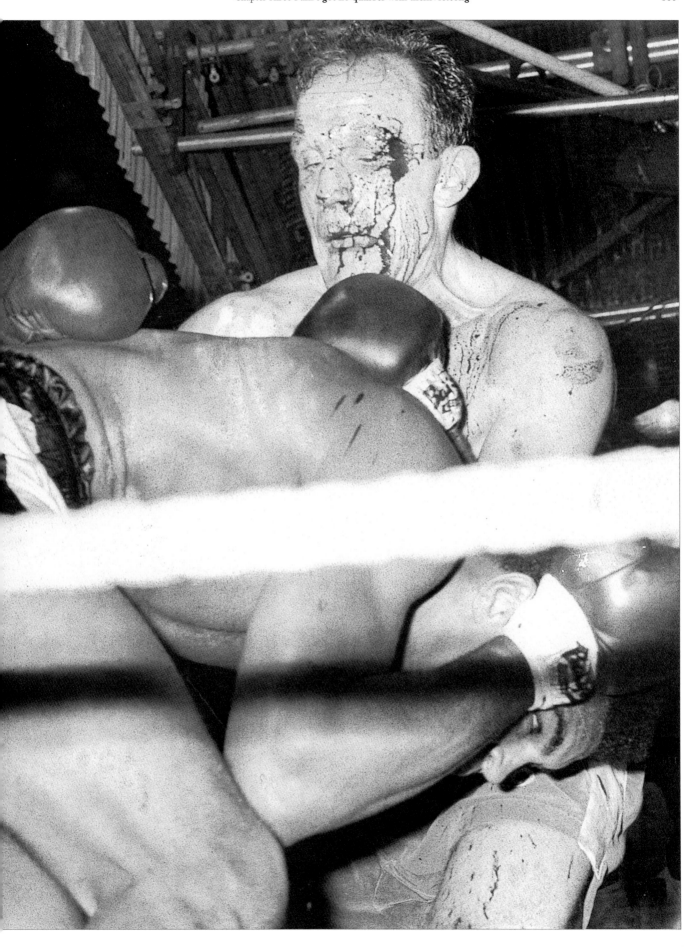

Ali throws a long right towards Cooper, who is already
bleeding heavily from the cut above his eye. Ali said later that
it was obvious that the fight was over, so he concentrated on
defending himself until the referee stepped in.

An end to the challenge

Above: Referee George Smith stops the fight one minute and 38 seconds into the sixth round, because of the damage to Cooper's eye; Ali has retained his title.

Right: Cooper is escorted away from the ring to get medical attention; the cut requires twelve stitches. He said later, 'Ali didn't know too much for me. It was a physical thing that let me down - having prominent bones and weak tissue around the eyes.' Ali, by contrast, was almost unmarked as usual.

For the first time, Cooper's Italian wife, Albina, had seen him fight. Cooper had asked her to come because the fight was so important and he felt he would win, but she said afterwards that she had been very scared and would never attend another of his bouts.

Opposite: The champ at a Press conference held at the Piccadilly Hotel after the fight. He and a friend, black baseball player Jimmy Brown, had been subjected to racial abuse by four members of the audience as they left the ring, but they both brushed off the incident as unimportant.

Opposite: Ali eavesdrops as promoter Harry Levene announces to the Press that the gross income from the fight was £400,000.

Above: Ali plays a tune on the piano at the Press conference.

Below: On the Eamonn Andrews Show, Ali's fellow guests include Lucille Ball, Noel Coward and Dudley Moore.

'Everybody has been kindness itself'

Right: The Eamonn Andrews Show goes out late on Sunday night on Britain's ATV. The host and Ali share a joke.

Below: Ali looks thoughful as he watches a private showing in the West End of the film of his fight with Cooper. He said 'I have been overwhelmed with my reception in London. Everybody has been kindness itself. And Cooper! He's a real gentleman and a fine opponent.' Ali's earnings from the fight are estimated at £215,000, while Cooper is expected to get £40,000. Cooper has also been offered a further £16.000 for his life story, by a British newspaper

Opposite above: At the end of May 1966, Ali visits Egypt again, at the invitation of the Supreme Council of Islamic Affairs.

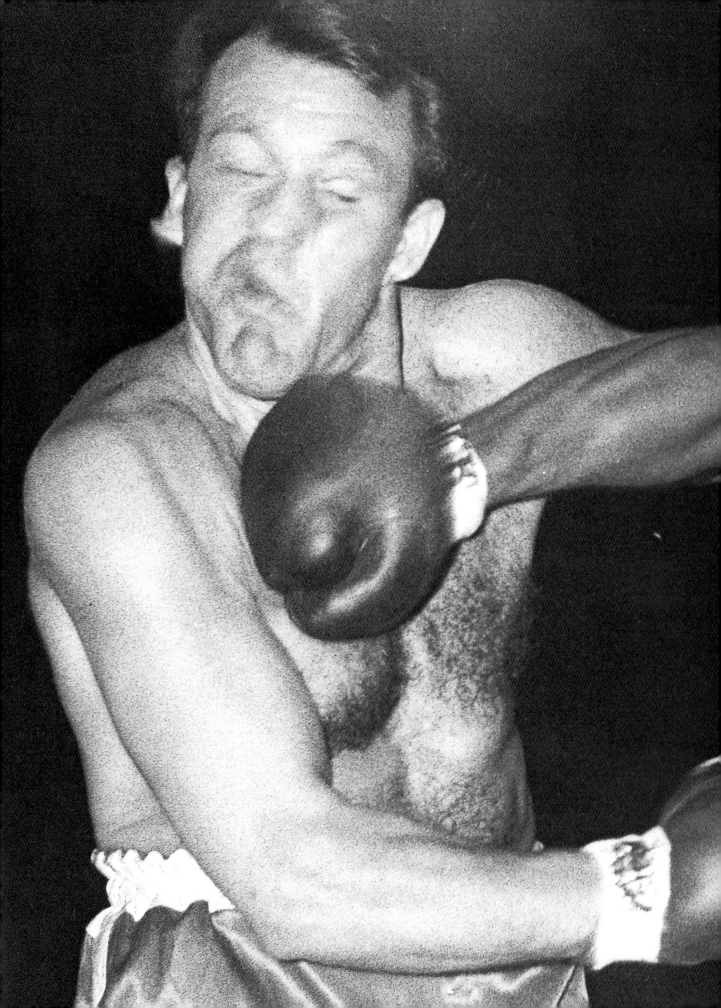

Chapter Four

'I don't have to be who you want me to be'

t the beginning of August 1966, Ali was back in Britain to fight Brian London, who he disposed of in only three rounds. Two months later, Ali's contract with the Louisville Sponsoring Group expired; he then appointed Herbert Muhammad as his new manager and the boxing world was appalled. Some believed that the money Ali made would now be used to finance the 'Black Muslims', although there was no evidence that this would happen. Elijah Muhammad did not approve of fighting for money and had sent his son to manage Ali only to 'keep the white man from defrauding' him. Despite their anti-white beliefs, the Muslims made no move to get rid of Dundee. He never got involved in Ali's political or religious activities - his job was to get Ali ready to fight and he stayed as trainer for Ali's entire boxing career.

In September, another title fight was held abroad, against Karl Mildenberger in Frankfurt. The bout became the first sporting event to be beamed in colour by satellite, but it also marked the last time Ali appeared on US network television for seven years. Partly this was due to the better profits that could be made using closed-circuit television, but it was also due to political pressure from government and advertisers.

Ali at last fought again on American soil that November, in Houston, Texas. His opponent was Cleveland Williams, once a really hard-hitting puncher who would have been a real problem for Ali, but now a shadow of his former self. The fight generated huge publicity because of the controversy around Ali, breaking records for the largest crowd of people to watch a boxing match live. Ali dominated the match from the start, finally earning a grudging respect from sports writers who had questioned his ability. He was in his prime and had proved once and for all that his skill in the ring was supreme.

At the beginning of 1967, Ali finally got to fight Ernie Terrell. After his virtuoso display against Williams, Ali was favoured - but many thought that Terrell would give him the hardest fight of his career. Terrell was at the height of his powers and was unbeaten in 15 fights over the previous five years. The pre-fight build-up quickly turned nasty, when Terrell referred to Ali as Clay. The boxing establishment and many of the Press were still refusing to use Ali's new name - and even those reporters who wrote 'Muhammad Ali' in their articles would usually find that some editor had changed it to 'Cassius Clay' for publication. Ali regarded being called by his 'slave' name as a major insult that he took personally. He announced that Terrell had sold out for the white man's dollar and that he intended to 'whup' Terrell until he was called by his proper name.

The fight was the most vicious and brutal of Ali's career. Early on, Terrell suffered an injury to his eye, which he later said he thought Ali had caused deliberately - although Ali denied it. Terrell began seeing double and couldn't fight properly, since he didn't know what to hit. From the eighth round onwards he was virtually helpless, but Ali continued to rain blows on him for a further seven rounds, continually shouting, 'What's my name?' Terrell wasn't listening - he was too busy trying to survive.

The respect for Ali's skills that had been felt after the Williams fight was largely forgotten in the aftermath of the fight with Terrell. The Press roundly condemned Ali's brutality and cruelty and his apparent defiance of the rules of sportsmanship and decency. Ali knew he had gone too far, but continued to deny that he had fought dirty. The fiasco couldn't have come at a worse time in terms of public opinion. Ali was still claiming conscientious-objector status and saying he was a man of peace, but he had beaten another fighter into a pulp in the ring. A month afterwards, the Appeal Board voted unanimously to uphold his 1-A classification and he was told to report for induction on April 11 in his hometown of Louisville. His lawyer had the date changed to April 28 in Houston, Texas, but after that there was little to do but wait.

As the days passed, anyone who supported Ali publicly was subjected to pressure groups, irate letters from war veterans and even death threats. In the light of later events his stand seems more understandable and even reasonable, but this was before the tide of opinion had changed on Vietnam, and many thought he should go and fight. Ali arrived at the induction centre early and the first half of the proceedings went ahead quietly. Then came the moment when he and the others were lined up and asked to step forward after their name was called, the step signifying that they were now inducted into the Armed Forces. When the officer called out 'Cassius Marcellus Clay', Ali did not move. The procedure was repeated, after he had been told that refusal was a felony, but he still declined to step forward. The media were then informed of his non-compliance, and told that further action would be taken. Within an hour - before Ali could even be charged with a crime, let alone convicted, the New York State Athletic Commission suspended his boxing licence and withdrew recognition of his title. All the other US commissions quickly followed suit. This effectively meant that Ali was not only no longer the world heavyweight champion, he also couldn't fight professionally in America.

Ten days later, Ali appeared before a federal grand jury in Houston to be formally charged and was released on US$5,000 bail. It was not until June 19 that his trial began and within just two days he had been found guilty of refusing to be inducted and given the maximum sentence by the judge - five years' imprisonment and a US$10,000 fine. The judge also ordered that his passport be taken away, which - since he was already unable to fight in America - effectively ended his boxing career for the immediate future.

Ali's lawyers began the appeal process straight away, so Ali was released on bail again. He was now under constant FBI surveillance, couldn't work at his livelihood and had no other means of making money. He continued to attend Nation of Islam meetings and studying the teachings of Elijah Muhammad. He also married for the second time.

After his divorce from Sonji, Ali had been devastated and it took him a while to recover - although that didn't stop him from becoming quite a ladies' man. He decided that his next wife would be a good Muslim, and Belinda Boyd fitted the bill perfectly. Her mother was a companion to Elijah Muhammad's wife, she was only 17 and had been brought up in the religion. She was devoted to Islam and dressed modestly but spoke her mind and was good company. At first she did not return his regard, but Ali kept on visiting her family until she agreed to marry him. Due to Ali's problems the young couple had little money, but for a long time they were very happy.

Soon afterwards, Ali discovered a new way to earn a living: appearing on the college lecture circuit. His initial two appearances were arranged by Jeremiah Shabazz, one of his first teachers in the Nation of Islam. Not long afterwards, Ali signed with a company that arranged speakers and began travelling regularly to college campuses across America. His lectures were based on themes important to him: the war in Vietnam; being stripped of his title; his current life; integration and segregation; black pride and money

versus principle. It may have looked like he spoke off the cuff, but in fact he worked hard on his speeches, learning by heart what he wanted to say. Often he turned out very different to what the students had expected but, as Ali had said himself after the first Liston fight, 'I don't have to be what you want me to be'. Many of them would become eligible for the draft and were sympathetic to his point of view, but there were also some hecklers. Ali learned to turn interruptions into jokes and take his audience with him. Belinda travelled with him and later said it was one of the happiest times in their marriage.

Meanwhile, left without a world heavyweight champion, one of Ali's former promoters started a new company and proposed an eight-man elimination contest in conjunction with the World Boxing Association to find a new champion. Jimmy Ellis emerged as the victor, but almost simultaneously Joe Frazier knocked out Buster Mathis and was crowned New York world heavyweight champion. The confusion was not resolved until Frazier beat Ellis in 1970, to unify the two titles. Ali took these developments in his stride; 'Everybody knows I'm the champion. My ghost will haunt all the arenas. I'll be there, wearing a sheet and whispering, "Ali-e-e-e! Ali-e-e-e!"'

At a Press conference for the London fight, Ali looks morose. 'I've got two fights in my mind and no heavyweight of the world should have that. I don't want to burn myself up.'

Previous page: Look out London, here I come! Ali surveys the capital from the top of the Post Office tower at the beginning of his second trip to England in 1966, to fight Brian London, Britain's No 2 heavyweight.

'There ain't no more fun in it'

Above: Ali signs autographs in a London street. 'There just ain't no more fun in it,' he had confided at the Press conference. 'There's nothing new and I'm used to it like going to work. It's the guys trying to beat me who get the most fun.' He is not only preparing for the fight against London, which is scheduled for August 6 at Earls Court Stadium, but also working towards a title fight with Karl Mildenberger in Germany the following month.

Right: Herbert Muhammad stands by, as Ali looks through fabric swatches to select the material for his new suit from Harry Helman.

Brian London's challenge

Opposite: Outside The Noble Art Gym in London's Havistock Hill, Ali pauses to sign a few autographs after a work-out session. He has been training for the London fight with professional thoroughness since his arrival in England, despite suggestions that he was treating London's challenge with contempt.

Right: Ali in pensive mode. There had been reports that London would try to win the fight with rough-house tactics. Ali responded; 'Every man who fights me is fighting for his life. I'll quit when the first man beats me. But if London wants to fight dirty anything he does wrong I can do wrong. I'll have to break a few rules.'

Below: Just before the fight, Ali took a break to visit his friend Jim Brown on the set of *The Dirty Dozen*, which was being filmed on location at Beechwood Park School in Markyate, Hertfordshire.

This is how it works...

Opposite: Lee Marvin shows Ali the workings of the automatic weapon he is using in *The Dirty Dozen*. Ali also met some of the other stars of the film, including Clint Walker and Trini Lopez.

Right: One of the managers of the Cumberland Hotel, Stuart Denny, accompanies Ali on an early morning training run in Hyde Park, London. Ali is staying at the hotel with his entourage.

Below: Ali works up a sweat in training. Meanwhile London had taken a break from sparring amidst reports that he was suffering from a muscle strain.

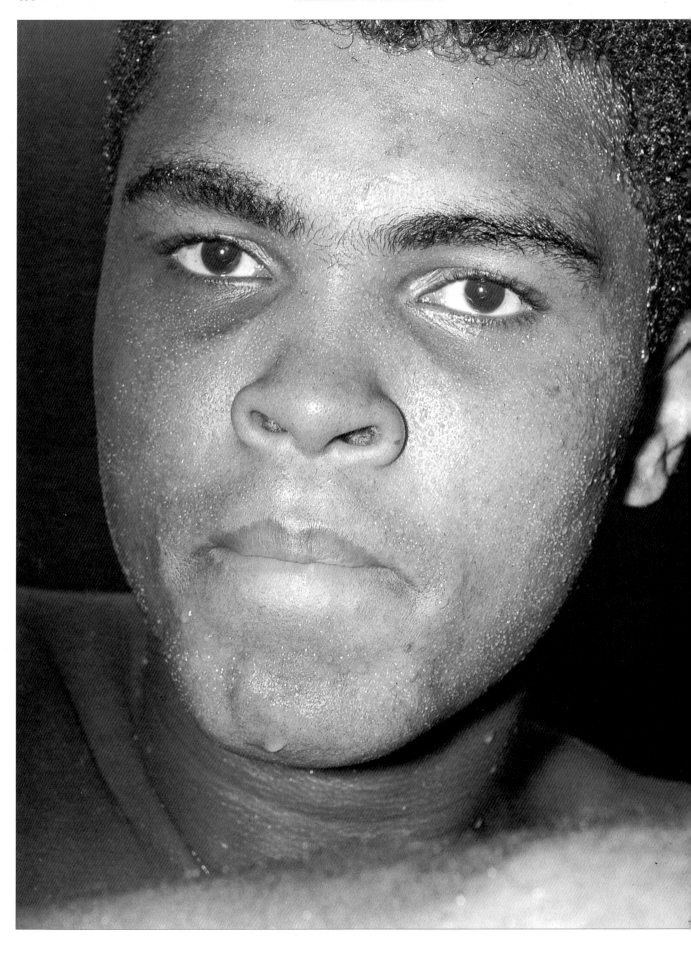

On with the training programme

Opposite: It shook a few theories about hair and manhood when the greatest-ever heavyweight revealed that at 24, he only shaves once a month. He told reporters, 'A razor company offered me a lot of dollars, but I just couldn't take them.'

Above: As part of his training programme, Ali bangs a heavy bag for the equivalent of five rounds.

Right: He also sparred seven rounds with partner Cody Jones, who had been selected as he was built along similar lines to London and moves forward in the same way. Although Ali had done some preparatory work in Miami, he had left serious training for the fight until his arrival in England.

'I'm getting old'

Ali continues working out in the ring. He told reporters, 'I saw London fight Patterson on television... I thought then that one day I would be champion. I was up this morning at five, running for miles and miles. I wish I'd seen a doctor on television when I was a boy, instead of a boxer. This is a hard way to make a living. I'm getting old.'

The world heavyweight champ was still having problems working up enthusiasm for the forthcoming fight. He had little respect for London's ability, but realized that the challenger would be trained for peak effort at Earls Court on the evening of August 6.

Reflex action

Opposite: Ali's lightning reflexes slide him out of trouble as sparring partner Jimmy Ellis throws a straight left, during their five-round work-out at The Noble Art Gym of the British Boxing Board of Control.

Henry Cooper watches with interest as Ali limbers up in the ring.

Ali takes time out from training to chat to his last opponent, who has come to watch the work-out. The two meet on genial terms, with no hard feelings about the result. Ali had gone round to Cooper's dressing room immediately after their bout to apologize for the cut that had stopped the fight. Cooper had said at the time, 'It was a pity. We was really enjoying ourselves. But I would have done the same to you if I could!'

Ali shakes hands with Brian London at the weigh-in for the forthcoming fight. Between the two boxers stands promoter Jack Solomons.

Weight-watching

Opposite: The champ weighs in at 209½lbs for the fight - eight pounds heavier than when he had fought Cooper nearly three months previously.

Right: Ali watches in the background as London is weighed. The challenger scales at 200½lbs.

Below: The fight begins and is broadcast live on BBC radio from 10.15 p.m. onwards. It is also beamed live to televisions in America, but in Britain can only be seen on CCTV in cinemas. London is quickly outclassed, as Ali hammers a right to the head and his opponent almost sinks to the canvas.

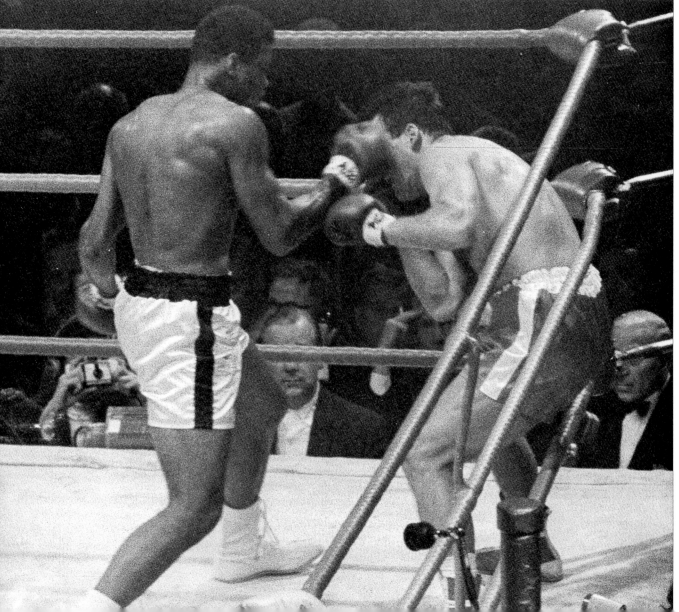

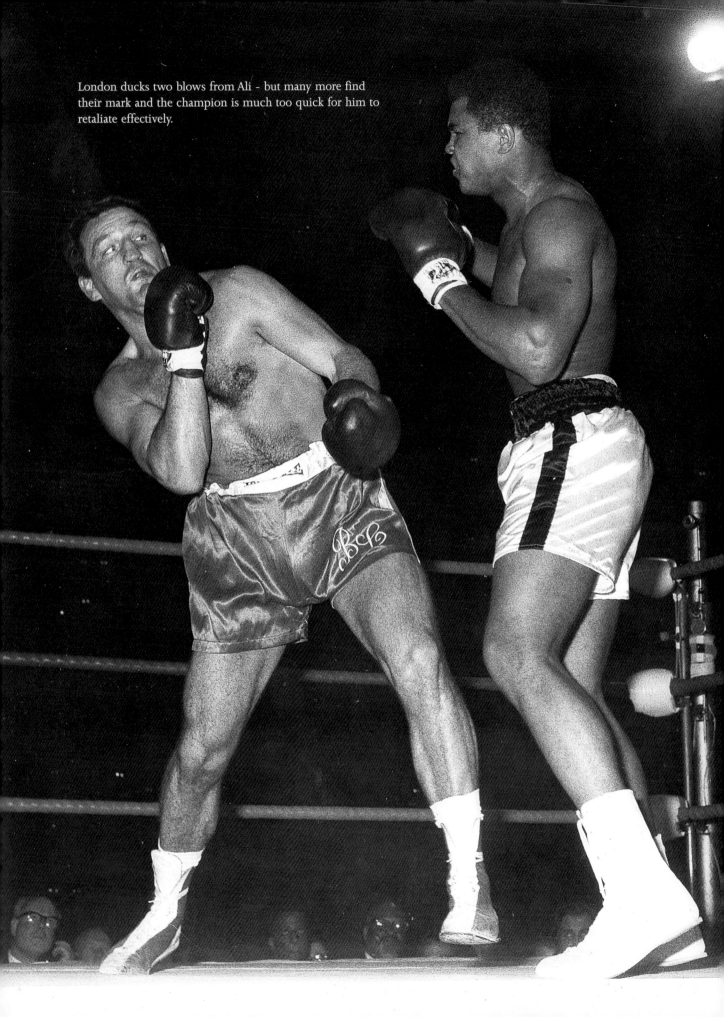

London ducks two blows from Ali - but many more find their mark and the champion is much too quick for him to retaliate effectively.

It's a knockout!

Opposite and right: Ali flattens London with a killer right one minute and 40 seconds into the third round and retires to a neutral corner as referee Harry Gibbs begins the count. Gibbs spreads his arms to signal that it is a knock-out, as a prone London still struggles to get to his feet. London said afterwards, 'I went into the ring expecting to go the full 15 rounds. I reckon I'm as good as the rest. But Ali is different. He's more than the greatest. Everything happened so quickly; I don't know what punch actually got me.'

In Ali's dressing room later, London said to the champ, 'I'd like a return match, but only if you put a 56lb weight on each ankle.'

Below: Ali, with Herbert Muhammad, is interviewed after the fight. Ali's contract with the Louisville Sponsoring Group is shortly to run out and there is an uproar in the world of boxing when he appoints Muhammad as his new manager. Sporting pundits saw it as another move away from the establishment, or as the 'Black Muslims' attempting to wrest control of the fight business - and all its money.

The champ goes home

Opposite above: Ali waves to the waiting crowd as he leaves his hotel the day after the London fight, on his way to the airport to fly home to America. There he was due to appear at a special hearing later in August, to consider his claim for conscientious-objector status. Against all expectations, the judge recommended that his religious beliefs were sincere and that his claim should be sustained.

Opposite below: Ali at a Press conference with Joe Louis and Karl Mildenberger, a few days before he is to fight Mildenberger in Frankfurt, Germany. Despite the friendly faces, there was still a rift between Ali and Louis over Ali's high-profile membership of the Nation of Islam and his refusal to fight in Vietnam.

Righ: Ali training at a Frankfurt sporting school before the bout with Mildenberger, which is scheduled for September 10, 1966.

'I fought my best...'

Opposite: Mildenberger checks Ali's weight before the fight. British referee Teddy Waltham was paid for his services in cash by the promoters, but later his pocket was picked and he lost the lot. Ali came to hear of it and replaced the money out of his own pocket.

Above: Mildenberger is sent to his corner by Waltham, after the referee had stopped the fight in the twelfth round. Ali raises his arms in triumph; he is awarded the decision on a technical knock-out, which meant he had retained his title yet again.

Left: Ali surrounded by well-wishers immediately after the fight. Mildenberger said of the evening's events, 'I fought my best... When he put me down in the tenth, that was when I knew I was in serious trouble.'

Five to one favourite

Back in America, Ali took on Cleveland 'Big Cat' Williams in Houston, Texas - the first championship fight he had fought on American soil for nearly a year. Before he was shot over a traffic violation, Williams had been an awesome fighter, but now he was no longer really a worthy opponent. Over 35,000 people attended the fight, in which Ali was five to one favourite. He dominated the fight from the start, knocking Williams down four times and never being touched himself. The referee finally stopped it in the third round and Ali was awarded a technical knock-out. He was perhaps at his best that evening, bold and young and demonstrating a strength and breathtaking skill that forced even his detractors to regard him with respect.

Opposite: Training for the fight against Terrell.

Opposite: At a Press conference before
the fight against Ernie Terrell, Ali called on
British journalist Peter Moss to try and block
his punches, so he could demonstrate how he
would win. The fight was predicted to be
close, as Terrell was the most dangerous
opponent Ali had faced since he had beaten
Liston three years earlier. Terrell was taller and
had a longer reach, but the two fighters had
been sparring partners in Miami in 1962 so
Ali was used to his style and was confident he
could win.

Above and right: The fight was savage and in
one of the early rounds, Terrell suffered a
broken bone under his left eye, which he later
said Ali had caused deliberately by pushing his
thumb into the eye and rubbing it along the
top rope. The injury was not particularly
painful, but it caused Terrell to develop double
vision, which hampered his ability to fight.
Films of the bout did not reveal the cause of
the damage and Ali vehemently denied any
wrongdoing - although he admitted he had
been very angry with Terrell and had tried to
force him to say 'Muhammad Ali'.

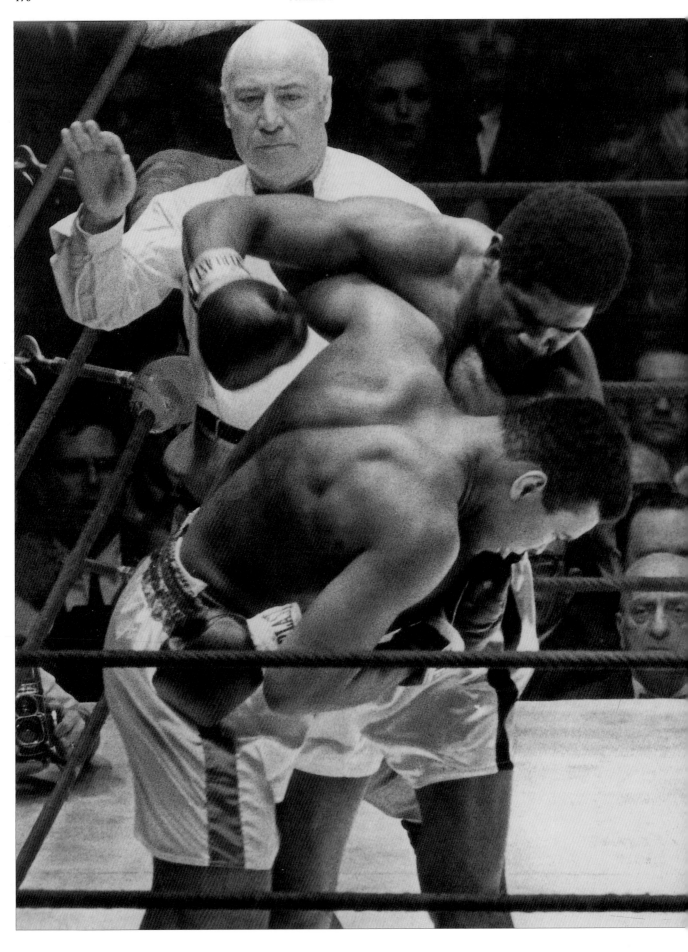

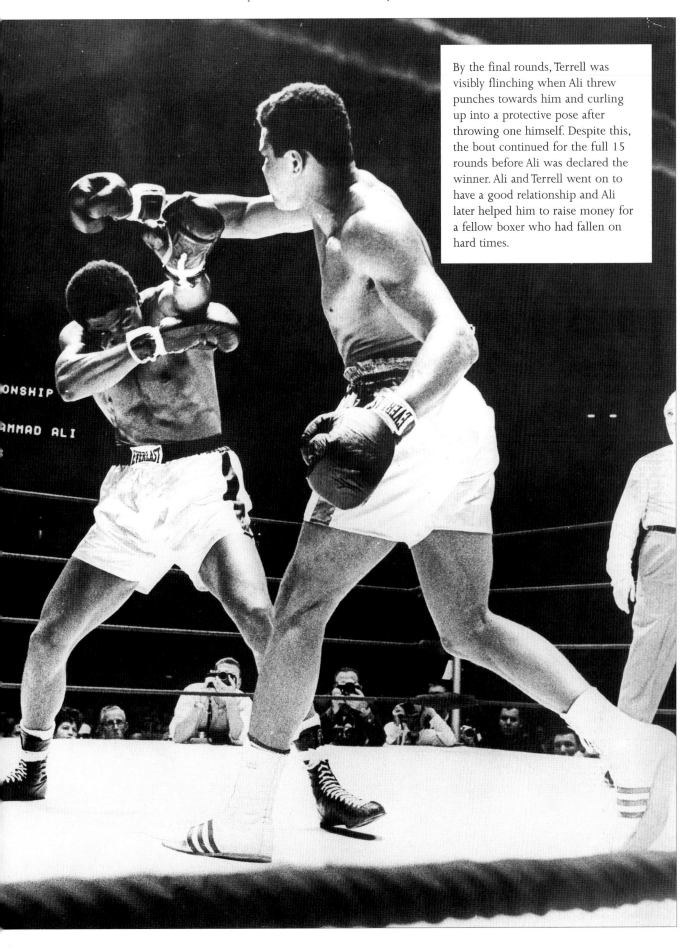

By the final rounds, Terrell was visibly flinching when Ali threw punches towards him and curling up into a protective pose after throwing one himself. Despite this, the bout continued for the full 15 rounds before Ali was declared the winner. Ali and Terrell went on to have a good relationship and Ali later helped him to raise money for a fellow boxer who had fallen on hard times.

Always the champ

Opposite and above: On 22 March, Ali fought his last championship bout before he was due to report for induction in the US armed forces. It was staged at Madison Square Garden in New York - the first championship fight to be held there for 16 years - and was watched by more than 13,700 fans. The challenger was Zora Folley, a respected fighter from Arizona who was not seriously expected to take the title. Ali knocked him out in the seventh round with a right to the chin and Folley later said the blow was so fast that he didn't see it coming.

Right: After refusing to go into the army, Ali became a political symbol for all those against the war in Vietnam. He had given up everything for his beliefs, but he later said it had not been a sacrifice because he believed that what he was doing was right. Although he was unable to fight professionally, he still loved to spar with local children outside his home in Miami; to them he would always be the champ.

Chapter Five

'I'm fighting for my freedom'

n 1968, Belinda and Ali had their first child, a girl called Maryum, but this piece of good news was offset by hearing in May that the Fifth Circuit Court of Appeals had affirmed his conviction. At the end of the year, Ali was sent to prison for ten days – not for anything to do with his ongoing legal battle, but for driving without a valid licence in Florida. Ali had never been locked up before so prison was quite a shock, even though it was only for a short period, but he said he was prepared to go back inside for what he believed in, if he had to.

The college lecture circuit was enjoyable and Ali found it much easier than boxing, but he was still fighting to have his conviction overturned and the money he was earning was not enough to pay the mounting legal bills. During the course of a television interview he was asked if he would return to boxing, and said he would if the money was right. Elijah Muhammad had never approved of fighting for money, but had understood that it was Ali's means of earning a living and had allowed him to continue. After Ali was prevented from boxing, Muhammad thought there could be no need for him to return – his brothers in the Nation of Islam would take care of him and he could use his fame to publicize their cause. Now here Ali was saying he would go back for money, and to Muhammad that was tantamount to saying he would give up his religion if the price were right. His reaction was to take back the name he had given Ali and dub him Cassius Clay again and to suspend him from the Nation of Islam for one year. He could no longer take part in their religious activities and other members were forbidden to talk to him. Despite this, Ali was so popular that many members stayed in contact; eventually the fuss died away and although Muhammad made no public statement, Ali quietly returned to the fold.

There still remained the problem of money, however, so Ali involved himself in a series of projects to raise more funds. One was a documentary film, *AKA Cassius Clay*, which was eventually released in cinemas just before Ali returned to boxing in 1970. Another was a computer-generated fight between Ali and retired champion Rocky Marciano. This was created by filming the two of them fighting a series of one-minute rounds, some of which Ali won, others that Marciano won. The film was then fed into the computer, which compared the fighters on various characteristics and predicted the probable result, so that a film of a complete fight was produced. When this was screened in America, Marciano knocked Ali out in the 13th round, but this caused such uproar in Europe that a revised version was made for the BBC to broadcast in the UK, in which Ali beat Marciano on cuts. The whole thing was rather ridiculous, but it paid Ali $10,000 plus a percentage, which was a useful boost to his finances. Another venture into acting was to take the title role in a Broadway musical, *Buck White*. His performance surprized the drama critics, who were impressed by his dignity and musical singing. Ali himself didn't much like the experience - he said he felt like a tiger in a cage.

Meanwhile, America was slowly but surely turning against the war in Vietnam and public opinion was beginning to swing Ali's way. Ali had not been able fight in his home country because none of the state athletic commissions would issue him with a licence, but finally someone realized that in Georgia there was no state athletic commission. Political strings were pulled and a bout against Jerry Quarry was arranged in Atlanta, although the state governor was strongly opposed to the idea. After three years out of the ring, Ali was subdued about his chances: 'It's been so long… I'm fighting for my freedom'. In the first round he came out fighting, but in the second he had started to slow down and Quarry hit him with a brutal hook to the body. In round three he opened up a deep cut over Quarry's eye and the fight was stopped. Ali had won - but it was apparent he no longer had the speed and stamina of the past. Six weeks later Ali fought Oscar Bonavena in New York. The New York commission had been forced to back down after court action was taken against them for discrimination; Ali's lawyers were able to submit a long list of convicted felons who had been granted a licence despite their crimes. The fight was rather boring, but finally Ali hit Bonavena with a great left hook that caught him square on the chin and it was this moment of drama that people later remembered. Now he wanted to go after Joe Frazier and regain his title while he still had the chance.

For the first time, two undefeated heavyweight champions were fighting to decide who should have the world title. Ali had no personal grudge against Frazier, but he labelled him an 'Uncle Tom', said he had sold out to the white power structure and called him dumb and ugly. Perhaps Ali was releasing all the anger and frustration of the previous years, but Frazier was not as gifted with language and found it hard to retaliate effectively. He never forgot or forgave some of the insults, but he had his revenge. Ali had recently fought two bouts after three years out of training and he had not had enough time to recover or prepare. The fight was a close match and although Frazier knocked Ali down several times he always sprang up well before the count. However, at times Ali leaned against the ropes to rest and took punches, losing points that he would need later on. The fight went the full 15 rounds and at the end Frazier had won. Ali was philosophical about it: 'Just lost a fight, that's all'. One of the reporters said that Frazier believed Ali would not want to fight him again. Ali didn't hesitate: 'Oh, how wrong he is.'

Ali had shown that he was courageous and how well he could take a punch, but for the first time he had to rest and regain his strength. At this low period some good news did arrive - the Supreme Court reversed his conviction, so he was free from the threat of prison and was able to have his passport back. Over the next couple of years he travelled round the world, fighting exhibition matches and professional bouts, always winning and preparing himself to win back his title. He finally realized a dream and opened his own training camp, at Deer Lake, Pennsylvania - something he had wanted since his brief period at Archie Moore's camp in 1960. In many ways his camp was modelled on Moore's, with the names of famous boxers painted on large rocks in the grounds, and he continued to train there for the remainder of his career. Unlike those of many other fighters, Ali's camp was open house and visitors were always welcome. He was particularly fond of children and was always happy to spend time with them showing off his magic tricks - one of his favourites was to appear to levitate three inches off the ground.

Ali had been working towards a rematch with Frazier, but in 1973 George Foreman beat Frazier to take the title. Now to prove to everyone that he was the greatest he had to take on both men, but in March 1973 he suffered a setback when Ken Norton broke his jaw. Ali had been overconfident about the fight and not trained sufficiently, and a sprained ankle hampered what training he had done. The break was clean, but his jaw had to be wired up for six months, temporarily silencing him, which he later said was the worst punishment of all. Some thought perhaps this was the end of the line for Ali, but he fought Norton again after his jaw had mended and this time he won. Now he was ready to go after Frazier and Foreman.

Opposite: English artist Sarah Leighton meets Ali for the first time in London in 1971, as she prepares to paint his portrait.

Previous page: Ovaltine sponsored a trip to Nigeria, Italy, Switzerland and England in 1971. Ali was greeted by crowds at Heathrow airport and received the full red-carpet treatment. He stayed in London for several weeks, fighting exhibition bouts and attending celebrity events.

Right: In 1970, after more than three years of
exile, Ali was finally granted a licence to fight
Jerry Quarry on October 26, in Atlanta, Georgia.
The State Governor was against Ali fighting and
tried to invoke a state ordinance dating back to
just after the Civil War, which prohibited bouts
between blacks and whites. For a while things
hung in the balance, but finally were resolved.

Below: The auditorium was packed with boxing
fans, members of the black community, civil
rights leaders and movie stars who had come to
see Ali's return. Quarry was a top-rate fighter
and also the first younger man whom Ali had
faced as a professional, so the fight was expected
to be hard. In the first round, Ali was full of
energy and dazzled the audience with his
familiar display of speed, rushing round the ring
throwing punches, most of which landed.

Opposite: Although Ali slowed down in the
second round, he was still physically strong and
able to land punches. Quarry caused
consternation in the Ali corner when he landed
a tremendous hook to the body, but Ali still had
his ability to recover quickly from such blows
and he fought back strongly. In round three he
opened a bad cut above Quarry's eye and referee
Tony Perez stopped the fight.

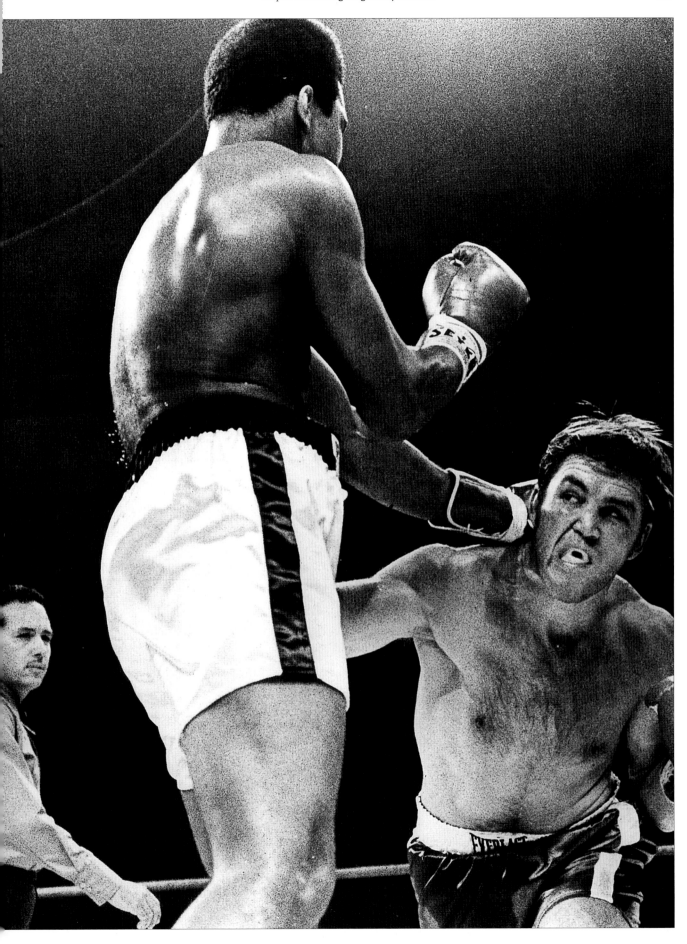

A chance at the champ

Above: At last Ali got the chance to win his title back, when a fight against Joe Frazier was set for March 8, 1971. Frazier had dropped out of school to work in a slaughterhouse, before winning a gold medal at the Tokyo Olympic Games in 1964. His fee for this first fight with Ali was US$2,500,000, an unheard-of figure in those days - and his opponent got the same.

Right: In a Press conference the day before, Ali said, 'People want to see me whipped because I'm arrogant, because of the draft, because of my religion… But I thrive on pressure. If there's no controversy, I can't get ready.'

Opposite above: The 'Fight of the Century' attracted a live audience of over 20,000, with millions more watching on television around the world.

Opposite below: After the first few rounds, Ali could no longer dance at speed and Frazier found he could land his punches. Ali rallied again towards the end, but in the 15th round Frazier landed a wicked left hook that sent Ali crashing towards the ropes.

Defeated!

Right: As Ali lay on the floor, Frazier was led to a neutral corner by referee Arthur Mercante - but by the time Mercante turned to pick up the count Ali was already on his feet. He managed to survive until the end of the 15th round, but the fight went to Frazier. Ali was not bitter about his defeat, 'Just lost a fight, that's all… There are more important things to mourn than Ali losing a fight. I'll probably be a better man for it.'

Below: When the result was announced the crowds went wild and police officers had to prevent fans from climbing into the ring. Both fighters had suffered damage to their faces - Frazier was bruised and swollen and Ali was taken to hospital with a suspected broken jaw. The x-rays were negative and Ali refused to stay in overnight for observation, because he didn't want people saying Frazier had put him in hospital.

A whim of iron

Right: Ali was determined to get his title back, but after the Supreme Court reversed his conviction he was no longer in danger of losing his license again, so was able to take things more slowly and prepare properly. He fought exhibition matches on a regular basis, and then in July 1971 took on his old sparring partner, Jimmy Ellis, who was the current WBA champion. Ali knocked him out in the 12th.

Below: Henry Cooper and Ali meet in London for the first time since their fight in May 1966. Ali was half an hour late; when asked when he would arrive, one of his aides said, 'It depends how he feels - he has a whim of iron'. Ali immediately spotted his old opponent and pretended to stalk him before asking when he was going to make a comeback. Cooper retaliated by challenging Ali to a game of golf - his new sport.

Guest of honour

Ali shapes up to Jack Bodell, the British and Empire heavyweight champion, at a dinner given by the World Sporting Club in London on October 18. Ali was guest of honour for the evening.

Opposite: In an exhibition staged at London's Hilton Hotel on October 10, Ali fends off Alonzo Johnson. The bout was part of the entertainment for the Anglo-American Sporting Club's ladies' night, and Ali was paid UK£4000 to appear..

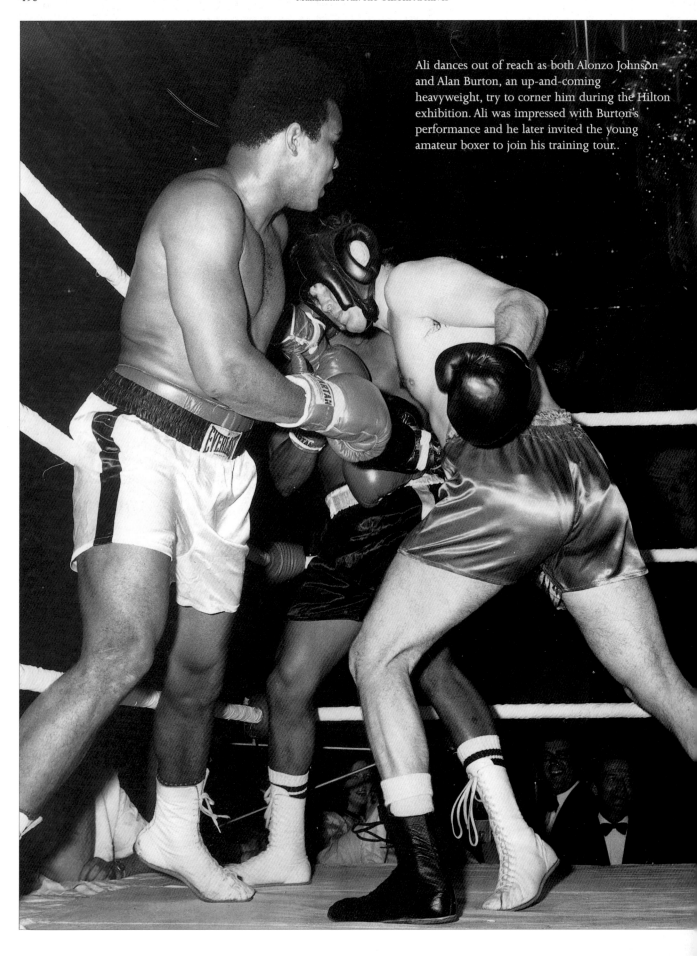

Ali dances out of reach as both Alonzo Johnson and Alan Burton, an up-and-coming heavyweight, try to corner him during the Hilton exhibition. Ali was impressed with Burton's performance and he later invited the young amateur boxer to join his training tour..

At an exhibition at London's Albert Hall on October 19, Ali is floored by Alan Burton. The fall was staged for photographers as part of the show.

Below: Johnny Frankham, Southern Area Light-heavyweight champion, gets his turn at flooring Ali.

Not so fast, Daddy!

Left: While in London, Ali was invited to appear at a lunchtime question-and-answer session at the London School of Economics. The event was arranged by the LSE's Islamic Society, but the hall was also packed with students who just wanted to hear Ali speak.

Below: Leaving London with his wife Belinda, Ali looks thoughtful as he contemplates his forthcoming schedule. He still has to appear at two exhibitions in Buenos Aires - and the fight with Buster Mathis in Houston was less than a month away. In the event the Mathis fight turned out to be very one-sided and Ali won easily.

Opposite: Ali combines family duties with his training schedule, by doing his road work while pushing his twin daughters, Rasheeda and Jamillah. His fight with German Jürgen Blin is only a few days away.

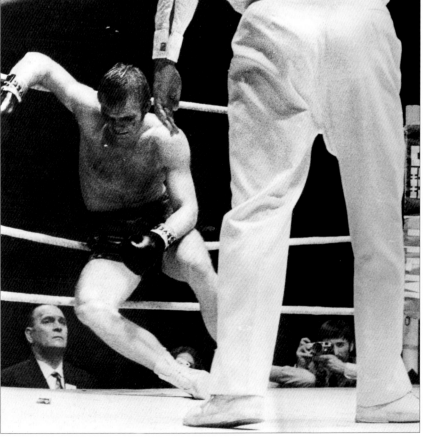

The 'Louisville Lip'

Above and left: The fight with Blin took place in Zurich at the end of December 1971. Most European heavyweights were not in Ali's class and Blin was no exception. Ali ran rings around him and used the opportunity to demonstrate his skills - even landing a triple hook at one point. He had moves to escape anything Blin tried to throw and finally knocked him out in the 7th round.

Opposite above: Ali shows a more thoughtful side, outside the Royal Lancaster hotel in London. He was about to leave for Saudi Arabia, on his first pilgrimage to Makkah.

Opposite below left: One of Ali's nicknames was the 'Louisville Lip' and his ability to promote himself was one of his big assets.

Opposite below right: I'm the Greatest! The waxwork Ali in Madame Tussaud's in London raises his arms in triumph.

Ahead on points

Opposite: Ali in London before he leaves for Makkah. He later said he was not ready for the trip - he didn't appreciate the history of his surroundings and was disappointed that nothing there was Westernized. After he had studied Islam longer he made the pilgrimage several more times and it was much more meaningful for him.

Left: In Tokyo, in April 1972, Ali beats Mac Foster on points. Foster had been keen to fight Ali because he was an ex-Marine and a Vietnam veteran.

Below: Ali listens carefully to Bundini, who always had a suggestion to make about pre-fight publicity. Ali was still working towards a rematch with Frazier, and this time he was determined to win. In May he beat George Chuvalo again, this time in the 12th round, while a re-match with Jerry Quarry in June ended in a knockout in round seven.

Ali in Dublin

Opposite: Training before the crowd in Croke Park, Dublin where he fights Al 'Blue' Lewis. The fight was held in the open air and more than 7000 fans crashed the main gates to get in free. Ali had helped Lewis when he was fresh out of prison in 1968, fighting three one-round exhibition matches with him. This fight lasted 11 rounds before Ali knocked Lewis out.

Ali had recently become a father again, as his first son had been born two months previously. Although he and Belinda were still married and there were apparently no problems between them, Ali was now a confirmed womanizer and in 1972 he also gained a new daughter, named Miya, whose mother was one of his girlfriends.

Above: After a rematch with Floyd Patterson, reporters flock round Ali. The bout was held back in New York, and Ali had knocked Patterson out in round seven.

Right: After Patterson, Ali went on to fight light-heavyweight champion Bob Foster in November. The fight was memorable because for the first time Ali's face was damaged when Foster managed to open up a cut under his left eyebrow that needed five stitches.

Problems in training

Right: For nearly two years Ali had been working towards a rematch with Frazier, but two months after the Foster fight, he learnt that Frazier had lost the world heavyweight title to George Foreman. He now had to beat Foreman to get his title back, but he also still wanted to fight Frazier and win. Meanwhile a fight with Joe Bugner was set for Valentine's Day 1973, in Las Vegas. The odds on Bugner winning were 8-1, so Ali was not taking his training too seriously.

Below and opposite: While Ali was preparing to fight Bugner, one of his sparring partners, Tony Doyle, suddenly lost his temper and hit Ali with three sledgehammer blows in the face within the space of five seconds. Once, Ali would have snapped his head back and avoided the blows or brushed them off, but instead they stopped him dead in his tracks.

There was a good reason for Doyle's action; Ali had been clowning around and using his sparring partners as fall guys in front of those watching the training. He had also said recently that 'sparring partners are the lowest form of life', so Doyle's retaliation had 800 onlookers roaring with appreciation. It also raised questions in the minds of sporting pundits who had seen the incident, as they knew Bugner had flattened Doyle with no bother at all only the previous year.

Opposite: Ali looks thoughtful before the Bugner fight. To enter the ring, he wore a flamboyant, flowing, jewel-encrusted robe, with 'People's Champion' written across the back, but it was not his choice - the robe had been a gift from Elvis Presley, whom Ali had admired since he was a teenager.

Ali's training sessions had been open to members of the public, who were charged a dollar a time to come in and see him working out. The training sessions may have proved to be more exciting than the fight itself, which turned out to be very slow-paced. Bugner came out fighting but Ali had little trouble in dodging his punches - despite his slack attitude to the pre-fight preparation.

A few exciting moments enlivened what was a very slow-paced fight.

Ali had won nine professional fights since being defeated by Frazier in 1971, and his victory over Bugner was number ten. He said later that he started believing he couldn't be beaten, '…too many easy victories can ruin a fighter just like a long line of defeats. You start thinking your name alone will win. You forget all the sacrifices that go into winning.'

To outsiders, though, all the signs looked good for a crack at the world championship and his first fight with Ken Norton, a relatively obscure boxer, was widely regarded as just a step on the way. It was scheduled just a month and a half after the Bugner fight, on March 31, 1973.

Right: Former world light-heavyweight champion Archie Moore separates Ken Norton and Ali, during a verbal skirmish at the Press conference to announce their forthcoming bout at the end of March 1973. An ex-Marine, Norton had knocked out 24 rivals in 30 fights, but none were world-class so Ali was not expected to have too much trouble beating him.

Below: Unfortunately, Ali believed the pre-fight hype and did less than three weeks' training. He also managed to sprain his ankle while clowning around on a golf course, trying to hit the ball on the move. In one of the early rounds Norton broke Ali's jaw, but Ali refused to allow the fight to be stopped. He fought for 12 rounds, before judges declared Norton the winner.

Opposite: After 90 minutes of surgery on his jaw and six months' recuperation, Ali was ready for a rematch. At a Press conference before the fight he said, 'I took a nobody and created a monster. I gave him glory. Now I have to punish him bad.' This time Ali trained hard and although the fight was close and went to the 12th round, he won a unanimous decision.

Back in shape

Right: After Norton, Ali took on Rudi Lubbers in Jakarta, Indonesia on October 20, 1973. Again he trained properly for the fight, and went on to win in the 12th round. Afterwards he said, 'Lubbers is a good fighter. I hit him with everything I could.'

Opposite: Ali was now in pretty good shape, perhaps the best he had been in since his comeback. He was confident that he was ready for Frazier - and that this time he would win. After his fight against Lubbers, when asked why he had seldom thrown a right, Ali said, 'I'm saving it for Joe Frazier.' The rematch was already set for January the following year..

Above: Ali tames a lion cub.

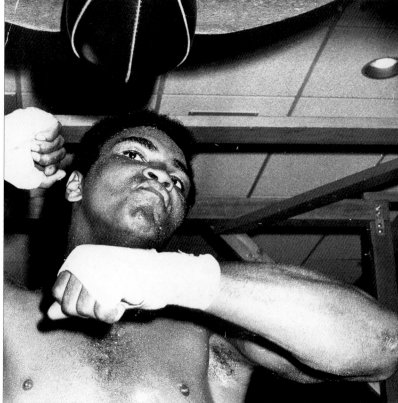

Proud of the punishment he could take...

Ali's Deer Lake training camp. The camp was based on that of Archie Moore, where Ali had briefly trained when he first became professional. Scattered around the grounds were large boulders, each painted with the name of a famous fighter - an idea he had copied from Moore.

Opposite: Although he was in great physical shape, it was obvious that the three-year lay-off and his age were beginning to tell on Ali - blows that he would once have brushed off or danced away from were beginning to land. Instead of glorying in his ability to dance away from danger, Ali was now beginning to become proud of the punishment he could take.

Chapter Six

'His hands can't hit
what his eyes don't see'

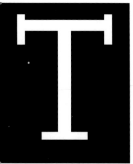he rematch against Frazier was again fought in New York, at Madison Square Garden, but just a few days before Ali and Frazier became involved in a brawl on television. They were in the studio together to comment on a film of their previous fight and all went well until Frazier mentioned that Ali had gone to hospital afterwards. Ali immediately jumped to the attack, pointing out that Frazier had been in hospital also and calling him ignorant. The two of them squared up and the situation quickly degenerated before others in the studio intervened. They were both fined US$5,000 by the New York State Athletic Commission but public interest in the bout was now at fever pitch. On the night the fight was fairly even and there was little controversy. The outcome was very clear - Ali was the winner. Frazier immediately demanded a rematch and Ali said he'd be happy to give him all the chances he wanted.

But first there was the little matter of winning back the world championship title. The fight against George Foreman, in Kinshasa in Zaire, was quickly dubbed the 'Rumble in the Jungle'. Zaire's President Mobutu Sese Seko was persuaded to part with US$10 million in return for his name and that of his country being spread across the globe, with further funding from a corporation in Britain. Each fighter was guaranteed a purse of US$5 million - more than Joe Louis, Jack Dempsey or Rocky Marciano had earned in an entire career. The deal faltered when Ali told reporters that anyone who didn't take him seriously would be cooked and eaten by Mobutu's people when they got to Africa; Zaire's Foreign Minister was on the phone immediately to point out they were not cannibals. The Zaireans also disliked the original fight posters, which featured the slogan 'From the slave ship to the championship', and they had to be quickly changed.

Ali arrived in Zaire several weeks before the fight and he and his entourage were accommodated in the presidential compound, which had its own Olympic-size swimming pool and even a small zoo. By contrast, Foreman was initially installed in an old army compound, although later he moved to the Intercontinental, and he soon realized that the whole country was behind Ali. He was very miserable in Africa and stayed in seclusion, making little secret of the fact that he would prefer to be back in America. Whatever Ali felt about Zaire privately, publicly he knew what was required. He told everyone how comfortable he felt there, how much he loved the country, how pretty the women were and continually praised his hosts and their achievements. The fight was originally scheduled for September 25 but arrangements suffered a major setback when Foreman was cut just below the eyebrow during a training session. The fight had to be postponed for six weeks while the injury healed, but both fighters were warned it would be 'unwise' to try

and leave the country in the meantime. The enforced wait was easier for Ali than for Foreman because at least he could carry on training.

The fight finally took place on October 30, at 4.00 a.m. to fit in with peak-time television audiences in America. Despite his popularity, many thought Ali had little chance of beating Foreman. He was now 32, while Foreman was only 26, and Foreman had beaten both Frazier and Norton, the two fighters who had recently beaten Ali, within two rounds. In three years and 40 professional fights, no one had lasted more than three rounds with Foreman, who was the most powerful puncher in the history of heavyweight boxing. But Ali had a surprise in store for everyone. It was assumed that he would dance around as usual, keeping out of Foreman's way until the champion tired, and then move in for the kill. Right away he did something different - the minute the fight started he rushed over and hit Foreman on the head. Afterwards he did dance around for the first round, but the ring was slow because the foam-rubber floor had been laid too early and had softened in the heat. Ali quickly realized that if he continued dancing his legs would tire, so he adopted a technique he used while training - he retreated to the ropes to rest and let Foreman punch away. He blocked and dodged many of the blows, landing quite a few of his own in the process, and managed to win three of the first four rounds. Foreman landed several hard punches in the following couple of rounds, but Ali treated them with apparent disdain and by round eight Foreman was obviously tiring. At this point Ali abandoned his 'rope-a-dope' technique and moved forward at speed to catch Foreman with a straight right to the chin that felled him. Ali was champion of the world once more.

Yet again there was some controversy about the decision; Ali's trainer, Angelo Dundee, was accused of loosening the ropes the afternoon before, to give his fighter an advantage. Dundee denied the charge - he said he'd actually tightened them up, but the heat and humidity had caused them to stretch again and the ring crew had failed to tighten them further just before the bout. Foreman himself came up with a catalogue of other excuses: the count was too fast; his water was drugged; he hadn't regained his form after the cut. But later he admitted that Ali had just outsmarted him, and said he was proud to be part of the Ali legend.

When he went back to America, Ali was treated like a homecoming hero, being named 'Fighter of the Year' by *Ring*, 'Sportsman of the Year' by *Sports Illustrated*, and awarded the Hickock Belt, which was given each year to the most outstanding athlete in America. To round off the year he was invited to the White House by Gerald Ford, partly because of the President's interest in sport, but also as a gesture towards healing the wounds of racial division and Vietnam.

Ali's next fight was pretty much a 'no-contest', against ex-Marine Chuck Wepner. It was memorable for the US$20 million lawsuit that the referee, Tony Perez, served on Ali afterwards. Ali had appeared on ABC's *World of Sports* and complained about Perez, accusing him of allowing Wepner to fight unfairly and ruling a knockdown when Ali said he had fallen. He also accused Perez of underhand behaviour for temporarily halting the second round of the Ali-Frazier fight in January 1974, giving Frazier several seconds to recover from a straight right that had left him staggering. In court sympathies were with Ali, and the jury ruled for him. The other claim to fame of the Ali-Wepner fight is that it was the inspiration for the film *Rocky*.

After Ali had beaten Ron Lyle in Las Vegas and Joe Bugner in Malaysia, he and Frazier met for their third contest. The venue was Manila, and the fight soon became known as the 'Thriller in Manila'. By this time Ali's entourage consisted of over 50 people, very few with a clearly defined job description. One of them did have a definite role, though - Veronica Porche, who had been Ali's mistress for nearly a year. Ali and Belinda were still married and by now they had four children, but he also had two further children by other women. Everywhere he went women threw themselves at him and until now Belinda had turned a blind eye to his womanizing. Unfortunately President Marcos took Veronica to be Ali's wife and no one dared correct him. This reached the papers in America and Belinda could no longer ignore the situation; she flew to Manila, marched into the hotel and confronted Ali, then turned round and went back home on the same plane.

As to the fight itself, many agree that it was one of the greatest in the history of the sport. In the early rounds Ali controlled the action, dancing and holding Frazier at bay, but Frazier rallied and went after Ali with solid left hooks. It looked as if he might prevail, but Ali summoned up reserves of strength and unleashed a barrage of punches in the last couple of rounds. Before the start of the 15th round, with Frazier reeling and unable to see punches coming because of a swollen eye, the fight was stopped. Ali was the victor, but said, 'Frazier quit just before I did'.

Right: Ali chops wood at his training camp at Deer Lake, Pennsylvania. After he stopped fighting, he retained the camp and it was later leased for one dollar a year to a home for unwed pregnant teenagers.

Previous page: Ali strikes a pose. He had the personality and charm to carry off even the most outrageous statements and he was always game for anything that would bring publicity. Each of his opponents became the butt of his humour and sharp tongue, but it was never meant maliciously and he expected them to retaliate in kind.

Open house

Above: Ali with his second wife Belinda and twins Rasheeda and Jamillah at Deer Lake. His family usually lived at the camp with him when he was in training, along with many of the entourage. It was also open to anyone else who wanted to call by and there was always a constant stream of visitors. The camp consisted of a group of log cabins set amidst woods on a steep hill, down a track off Highway 61. Apart from living quarters, one cabin contained a modern gymnasium, another a cafeteria-style kitchen, and there were also stables and a corral.

Left: Ali gives an autograph to a fan at Heathrow airport during a trip to London.

Opposite: Belinda Ali with Muhammad Jr at Deer Lake. The neighbours had initially been worried when Ali and his entourage moved in, but they were soon won over. The air at the camp was clear and fresh, there was a great view and Ali drank water and ate vegetables and fruit grown locally with no chemicals. He regarded it as a place where he could nourish his soul as well as his body.

That's my boy!

Opposite: Ali in training for his second fight with Frazier. Frazier had lost the world heavyweight title to George Foreman, but Ali was still determined to beat him to prove that he could. He trained hard and suffered a bruised right hand during preparation for the fight, for which he was given a cortisone injection on the night.

Above: Both of Ali's parents came to watch him fight Frazier. His father, Cassius Marcellus Clay Snr, was an artist and signwriter. He taught both his sons to paint, before they went into boxing, and had done murals for many of the Baptist churches in Louisville.

Odessa Grady Clay, Ali's mother, stopped living with her husband in the seventies, although it was not widely known and they often put on a show of togetherness in public afterwards. Their marriage had been stormy, because of Clay Snr's drinking and womanizing.

Right: Referee Tony Perez comes between Ali and Frazier in round two of their heavyweight fight in New York's Madison Square Garden. Ali won in round twelve and the stage was set for George Foreman and the chance to regain the world crown.

'Rumble in the Jungle'

Below: Ali addresses the Press at Kinshasa, Zaire, where he has come to prepare for his fight with Foreman, which was quickly nicknamed the 'Rumble in the Jungle'. Ali went to Zaire several weeks before the fight, along with an entourage of 35 family members, sparring partners, friends and people whose function was obscure and unspecified.

Left: Ali messes around for the benefit of waiting Press photographers.

Opposite top: President Mobutu Sese Seko had parted with ten million dollars to see his name - and that of his country - spread across the world. To the Press, Ali made much of being in a country run by black people - at a function at the presidential palace, he said, 'Mr President, I've been a citizen of the United States of America for 33 years and was never invited to the White House. It sure gives me great pleasure to be invited to the Black House.'

Opposite below: During the fight, Ali took everything that Foreman could throw at him with apparent disdain. He leant against the ropes, blocking and dodging and leaning away from punches - his 'rope-a-dope' technique - until Foreman tired and Ali was able to knock him out. Ali was the heavyweight champion of the world again.

Number One Fan

Right and below: Ali meets his greatest fan - father of four Paddy Monaghan, who lives in Abingdon, Oxfordshire. Monaghan, once an amateur welterweight, was now the full-time, unpaid organizer of Ali's British fan club and had travelled to both America and Canada to see Ali. He had named Ali the 'People's Champ' and had stood by him when everyone else thought he was finished, during exile and after the first Frazier fight.

Monaghan had travelled up to London to see Ali at his hotel, and said, 'There is nothing like Ali. He is the greatest boxer and one of the greatest men who has ever lived.' Ali replied, 'He's my Number One fan in England.'

Above: Ali's girlfriend, Veronica Porche, leaves their London hotel in November 1974. Veronica had entered a beauty contest in America to find girls to promote the Ali-Foreman fight earlier that year and had been one of those chosen to go to Zaire. She soon set her sights on Ali and they began an affair, which went on after they left Zaire. Intelligent and well-educated, Veronica was also beautiful and ambitious. She was soon more than just one of Ali's women, although he managed to keep their relationship a secret for some time longer. Belinda, Ali's wife, knew there was something going on, but she initially chose to ignore it.

It was also in 1974 that Ali's daughter Khaliah, was born; her mother was yet another of Ali's girlfriends. Ali loved both girls as much as his other legitimate children, but their existence was much less public.

Right: Ali at a Press conference in London. He had come to England for a five-day visit and planned to watch Joe Bugner, the European heavyweight champion, fight American Boone Kirkman at the Royal Albert Hall.

The 'Sportsman of the Year'

Ali looks serious at his Press conference in London. After his victory over Foreman, past problems and disagreements had been forgotten. He was no longer the black sheep of the boxing world, but was recognized as a great athlete and a brave man who had stood up for his principles, despite what it had cost him. Before meeting Foreman he had said it would be his last bout, but now he told reporters that he would go on until 'somebody is great enough to beat me'. By continuing boxing he could earn great sums for the Islamic cause, and do much for the freedom of blacks in America.

Opposite: Just in case anyone thought he was be mellowing, Ali strikes an aggressive pose for waiting photographers.

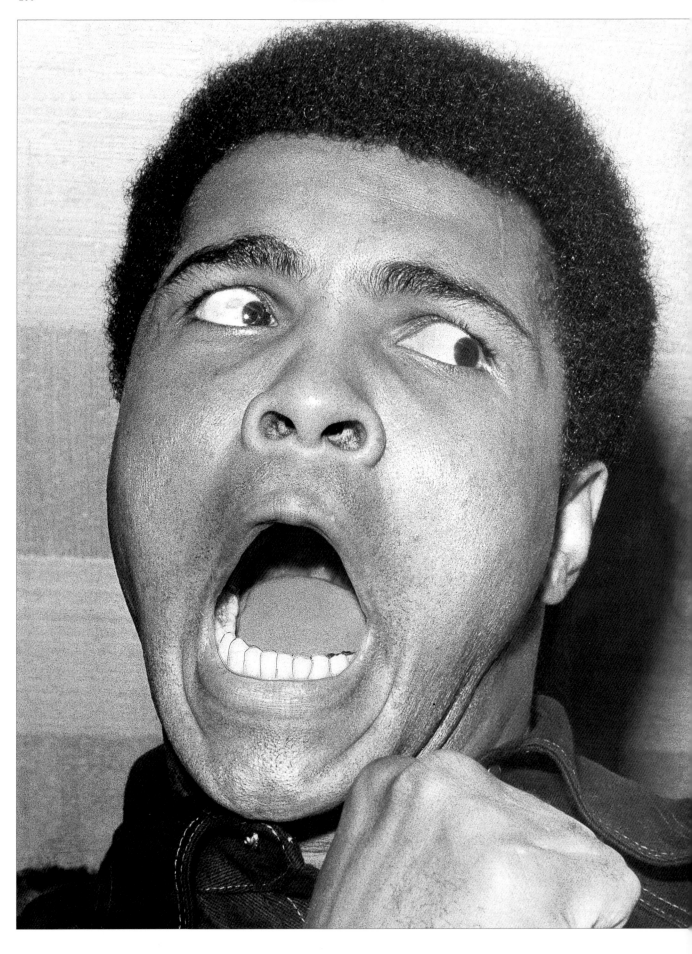

The right complexion, the right connexion...

Left: Ali could be quiet and reserved, but the minute there was an audience the loud-mouthed performer would appear. At his Press conference at the Hilton, he talked non-stop for 45 minutes, and assured reporters that Bugner was 'The best white fighter in the world and we still got a lot of racists about who want to see us fight. Bugner is the number four heavyweight in the world, the man's a top contender; he's got the right complexion and the right connexion.' Ali's top priority, however, was to fight Frazier and Foreman on the same night.

Opposite: Apparently, someone had offered him US$15 million if he could get both Frazier and Foreman into the ring against him. He planned to fight Frazier first over ten rounds, then go against Foreman without a rest. They would each earn US$5 million and would be able to retire.

Below: Ali on stage for a talk-in at the New Victoria Theatre in London.

A chat with the champ

Ali addresses fans at London's New Victoria Theatre.
They had come to hear him talk and to answer
questions, but the evening ended in a near-riot
when he came down from the stage to sign
autographs around the orchestra pit. The mania
quickly escalated to pop singer heights, with one
girl fainting as she was crushed against a stage
barrier, while another suffered a cut hand and torn
clothes. Boxing doctor Adrian Whiteson, who was
in the audience, volunteered to help the injured and
Ali rushed out of the stage door to avoid being
mobbed.

Meanwhile. he was in talks with Foreman, Frazier,
Bugner, Ron Lyle and Henry Clark over who should
be his next opponent. In the event it was none of
these - he actually fought Chuck Wepner, in March
1975.

Fleet Street's Number One boxing writer, Reg Gutteridge, makes a point to Ali. He had chaired the talk-in at the New Victoria Theatre.

Opposite above: At Tulse Hill Comprehensive School, Ali called for the tallest of the boys to come onto the stage. Tony Sibbliers, at 16 already six feet tall, came forward to engage in a one-minute sparring session with the champ.

Opposite below: Ali prepares to make a speech at the Anglo-American Sporting Club's dinner in his honor at the Hilton in London, in December 1974.

'Put 'em up, champ!'

Left: One of the kitchen staff at the Hilton is overjoyed to get a thank-you hug from Ali after the dinner in his honor.

Below: Ali also speaks to the chefs - one of whom gets a mock warning for his cooking.

Opposite above: Ali arrives at the Hilton in a Rolls-Royce, which has been put at his disposal during his visit.

Opposite below: Outside the Dominion in Tottenham Court Road, Ali is waylaid by Joe Bugner. Ali is due to watch him against Boone Kirkman on December 3, but Bugner is also keen for a chance at the world championship. It is eventually arranged that they will fight the following year.

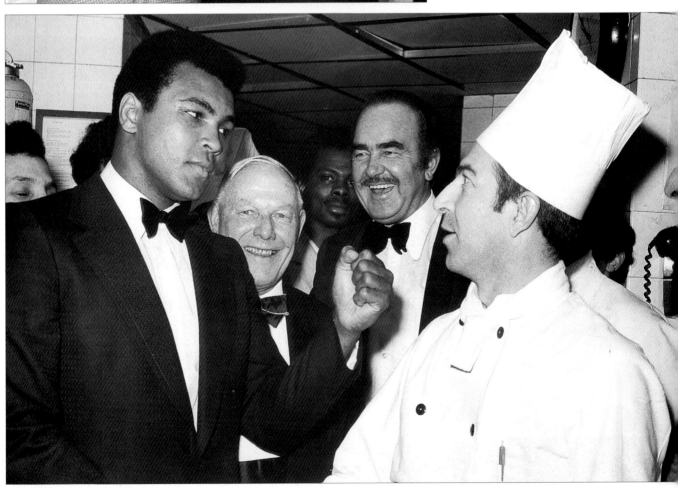

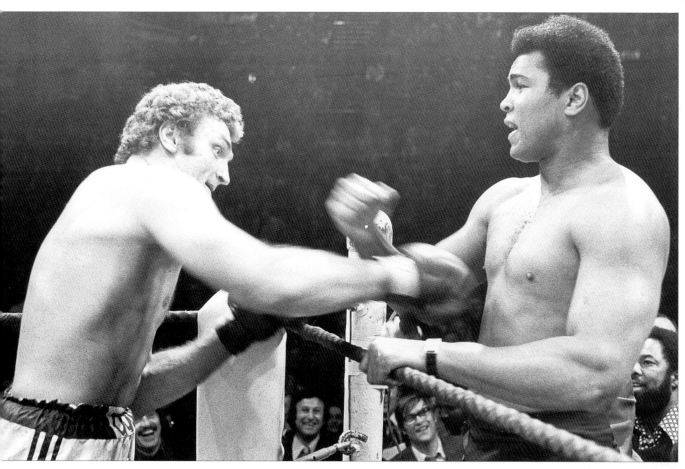

Opposite and above: Although Bugner had been due to fight Boone Kirkman, Kirkman had withdrawn just before the fight with a broken nose, which he had sustained when sparring with Frazier before he left America. With only a few days to go, the promoters had hurriedly substituted Alberto Lovell, an Argentinian who had never appeared in world rankings but who had a reputation as a big puncher. It was a disaster - Lovell was nowhere near Bugner in size or weight and boxed like a rank amateur.

The fight was stopped minutes into the second round, at which point Ali stood up at the ringside - where he was doing a spiel for BBC radio - stripped off his shirt and challenged Bugner through the ropes. The two of them engaged in a mock battle for a few seconds, to the amusement of the disappointed crowd.

Right: Oh no! Look, I got my name in the papers again! Ali checks reports of the fight in the London *Evening Standard*.

'We can't go on forever'

Opposite above: Ali and British up-and-coming boxer John Conteh discuss the fight business for the benefit of BBC Radio's listeners.

Opposite below: Dundee goes through a few points with Ali. He kept a detailed 'spy file' on possible opponents - which was often to lead to their downfall. Ali had recently fought Chuck Wepner and Ron Lyle in America, beating both.

However, a few days before the fight with Bugner in Malaysia, Ali announced he was '99% certain' he would retire afterwards and that he would name his successor on the morning after the fight. When he noticed tears in Dundee's eyes, he said, 'We can't go on forever.' Dundee replied, 'I think it's going to be dull for everyone.'

Right: Three days before the fight, Ali had sparred non-stop for 15 rounds, against two partners. It was both a psychological weapon against the Bugner camp, and to make up for several days of idleness in his roadwork.

Below: Bugner was in glowing good health, had a magnificent physique and skin that did not cut easily, but he was considered to be technically deficient - he had a good left jab, but few other punches and ducked his head when defending.

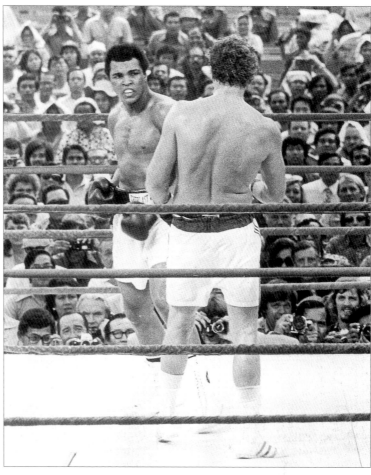

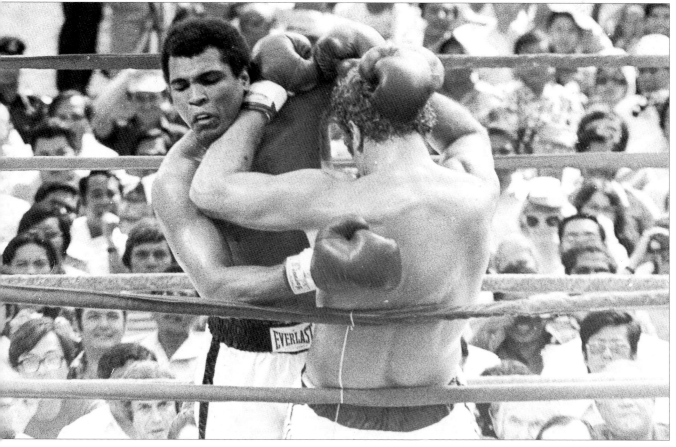

Right: For fighting Bugner, Ali was earning US$2 million - but the main draw for him was that the bout was being staged in a Muslim country. When he had talked of retiring, he told reporters that boxing would not be the same without a Muslim champion - there would be no more fights in Malaysia, Indonesia and Egypt; boxing would retreat to New York and its following would become limited.

Below: Ali was in great form, dominating the bout over all fifteen rounds, even though he had shown a distinct lack of dedication in his training. The climate may have been partly to blame - it was so hot and humid that even a short walk outside the air-conditioned hotel was like taking a shower.

Opposite: Even the British Press did not expect Bugner to win - they knew his shortcomings and thought the best he could hope for was to go the distance and lose honourably on points. And they were exactly right.

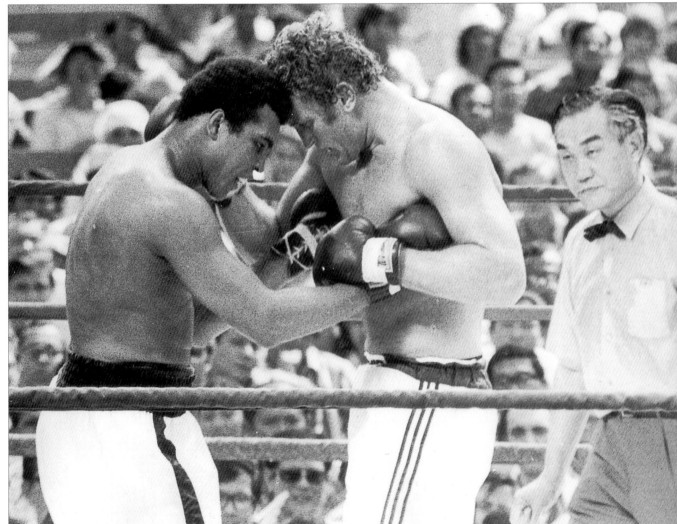

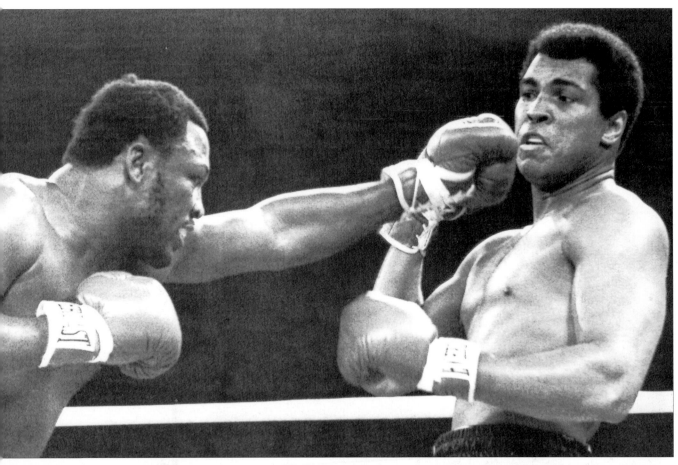

The 'Thriller in Manila'

As a finale to 1974, Ali fought Frazier one more time. Before the fight, Ali again went into his routine of pointing fun at and humiliating his opponent. He usually knew when to stop, but with Frazier he went too far several times and tensions between the two quickly escalated until it was evident that Frazier felt real hatred.

The fight itself unfolded like a three-act play. At first, Ali controlled the action and held Frazier at bay. In the middle of the fight, the tide began to turn when Frazier began to catch the champ with solid left hooks that bludgeoned him against the ropes. Although Ali apparently treated them with derision, he told Dundee, 'This is the closest I've come to dying.' Finally, Ali managed to call on his reserves of emotional and physical strength and unleashed a barrage of punches that sent Frazier reeling and closed his left eye. With limited vision he couldn't avoid further punishment, but he only surrendered when his chief cornerman refused to let him fight on.

Behind the scenes, another fight was brewing; when Ali went to Manila, Belinda had stayed behind with the children. Veronica had accompanied him instead and news of their relationship had now become public. Belinda was soon to take action.

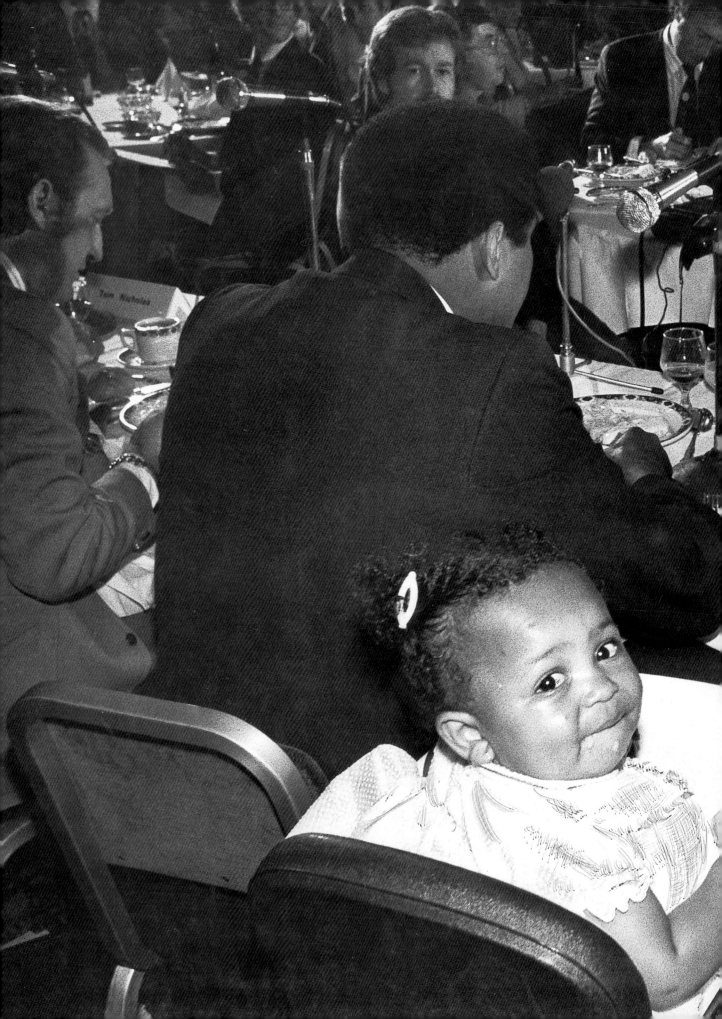

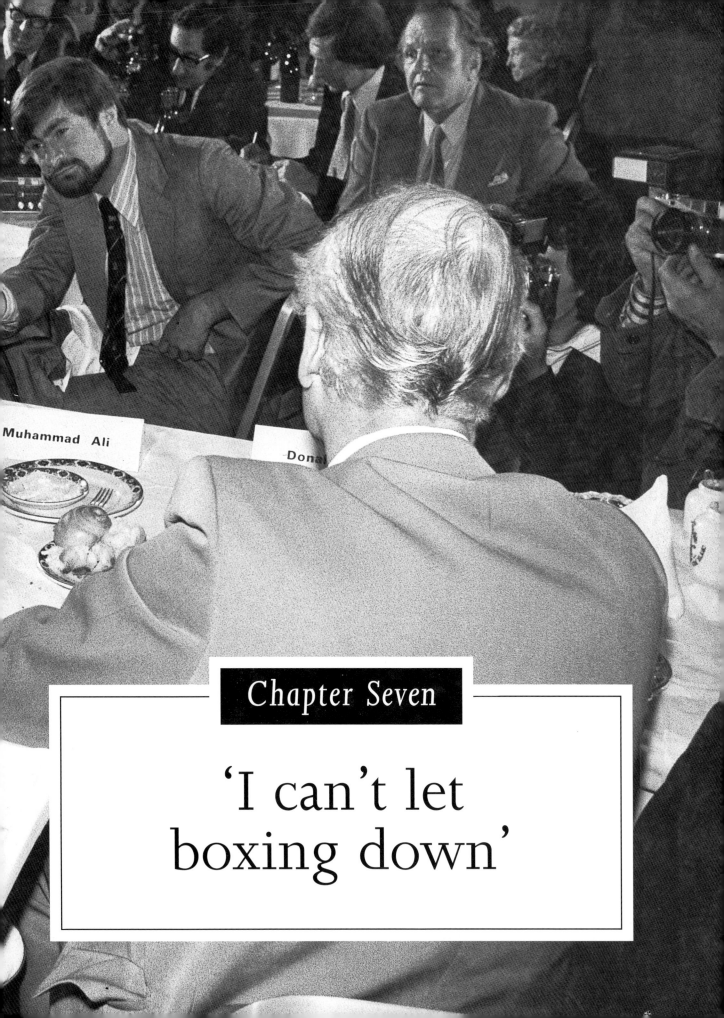

Muhammad Ali

Donal

Chapter Seven

'I can't let boxing down'

fter the third fight against Frazier, Ali said that he would like to retire. It would have been a good time for him to go - the fight had been exhilarating, he was admired and respected by much of the world, and although fighting was becoming hard work it wasn't yet too obvious. He didn't go through with it though: by February he was fighting Jean-Pierre Coopman, the 'Lion of Flanders'. It couldn't have been a much easier fight. Coopman was the Belgian heavyweight champion, but he was certainly not world-class and was so awed by fighting the great Ali that he just sat smiling at him throughout all their Press conferences. No one thought the bout would be competitive, but the venue was sold out and thousands more people turned up to watch on closed-circuit TV, just because it was Ali fighting. At the end of the first round, Ali joked with the TV network people that they wouldn't have time to get all their commercials in, but he managed to delay the finish into the fifth round. Ali's next fight, against Jimmy Young, was also supposed to be an easy one but Ali went into the ring out of shape and slow and although he won, it was not much of a show. He vowed to get himself back in shape for his third fight that year, against Englishman Richard Dunn in Germany. In the event the gate was poor, mainly because again no one expected it to be a fair contest. Ali took a cut in his purse in exchange for 2,000 tickets, which he handed out to American soldiers stationed in Germany. He said he thought they would want to see the fight, and that even though he didn't go into the army because of his religion, he had nothing against them for doing so. During the bout, Ali knocked Dunn down five times before finishing him off in the fifth round. Although he fought another seven championship bouts over the next five and a half years, these were to be the last knockdowns of his career.

Behind the scenes another fight was going on - Don King was making a bid to oust Herbert Muhammad and take over the management of Ali, something he had been planning since the 'Rumble in the Jungle'. King had already put several of Ali's entourage on his payroll, in return for reporting back to him and complimenting him to Ali whenever the occasion arose. Unfortunately for King, Ali had never much cared for him and he had vastly underestimated Ali's bond to Muhammad, so his bid for control failed.

During his career, Ali had often fought exhibition matches and his next fight in Tokyo was another of these - but a very unusual one. He was matched against Antonio Inoki, who was not a boxer but a Japanese wrestler. The promoters thought it would be interesting but in fact it was a disaster - Inoki was so terrified of Ali hitting him that he didn't wrestle at all, he just lay on his back kicking out to keep Ali away. Ali did manage to land several punches, but the bout was finally declared a draw. Unfortunately Inoki had kicked Ali's legs numerous times, badly bruising them and rupturing blood vessels. Instead of resting and getting proper treatment, Ali chose to continue with a planned trip to Korea and Manila and by the time he got back to America things were so bad he had to go into hospital to be treated for blood clots and muscle damage.

Meanwhile, Ali and Veronica were still together and in August they had a baby daughter, Hana. Not long afterwards he and Belinda finally filed for divorce - they had been married for nine years and she had supported him loyally, but enough was enough. The problems in his personal life did not stop Ali training hard for his next fight. This time no one expected it to be an easy ride - he was fighting Ken Norton for the third time. Norton had broken Ali's jaw during their first fight and come close to winning the rematch; now Ali was past his best while Norton was hungry for victory. In the early rounds, Norton had things pretty much his own way, but by round nine Ali was fighting back strongly and in the final round they were even. However, at this point Norton was advised by his corner that he was ahead and not to take chances, while Dundee told Ali to get out there and fight to win. Consequently, Norton gave away the early part of the round and Ali was declared the winner. Norton was furious - not with Ali, who he felt had fought fairly, but with the judges, who he accused of giving the match to Ali unjustly.

Except for a series of exhibition matches in January in Boston, Ali now took a rest for seven months and his next proper fight was another easy one. His opponent was Alfredo Evangelista, a Spanish fighter who had only been professional for 19 months. The contest provided ample proof that Ali was not as invincible as he had once been; Evangelista had never survived more than eight rounds before, but this bout dragged on for the full 15 rounds before Ali managed to prevail.

Despite his problems in the ring, Ali was still the best-known and most popular athlete in the world and there was tremendous interest in him and his life - even from those who were not fans of boxing. In 1976, Random House released his 'autobiography' - which had been written by Richard Durham, an editor for *Muhammad Speaks*. He was hampered by the fact that Ali showed little enthusiasm for the project, and was not willing to put in enough time and effort to really make something of it. The following year, Columbia Pictures released their film of Ali's life, *The Greatest*, a highly fictionalized account which starred Ali himself and several members of his entourage. It was not a good film - Ali being himself was still magnificent, but perhaps he had too much influence on how the film was made. Several other projects also came to fruition in 1977 - DC Comics licensed Ali's name and image for 'Superman vs. Muhammad Ali: The Fight to Save Earth from Star Warriors', and he also became the spokesman for an American household cockroach killer.

However much money Ali made outside the ring, he was still unable to walk away from boxing. At the end of September he was booked to fight Earnie Shavers, a bout that was predicted to be nasty because Shavers was another hard puncher - and now Ali was slower he was getting hit. Shavers could have won in the second round after an overhand right sent his opponent reeling, but Ali managed to pretend that he was only messing around so Shavers didn't press forward and consolidate his advantage. The fight was very close for the entire 15 rounds, but the final result was in Ali's favour. Afterwards, he said, '…my hands hurt, my knees hurt, my back hurts. I'm 35 years old. With the wear and tear I've been through, it's a miracle I did this for 15 rounds.'

It wasn't just Ali who was thinking along those lines. At a Press conference after the fight, Teddy Brenner - who had become increasingly concerned about Ali's health - announced that Madison Square Garden would not make any more offers to Ali while he was in charge; 'This is a young man's game… The trick in boxing is to get out at the right time, and the 15th round last night was the right time for Ali.' A week later Ali's physician, Ferdie Pacheco, who had been with him almost from the start, resigned. He didn't want to continue being part of the circus that was keeping Ali in the ring, particularly after a lab report revealed that the 'rope-a-dope' technique was resulting in increasing damage to Ali's kidneys. But the person who had to make the final decision to quit was Ali himself, and however much he may have thought about retiring a mixture of pride, money, love of the attention, and people's expectations was keeping him going.

Ali signing autographs in Paris in March 1976, outside the Crazy Horse Saloon in l'avenue George V. He had spent the evening watching the celebrated cabaret there.

Previous page: A hug for actress Annazette Chase, who plays Ali's second wife, Belinda, in the film of The Greatest, which was filmed at the end of 1976 and released the following year.

An American in Paris

Ali signing copies of his biography, The Greatest, at the launch of the French edition in March 1976 in Paris. A second book, I am King, telling his life in pictures and assembled by David King, was published at the same time.

Opposite: During his visit to Paris, Ali went to the salon of Pierre Cardin to see the spring/summer collection. As the models passed in front of him, journalists noted that he appeared very interested in women's fashion.

On to London

From Paris, Ali went to London via Amsterdam to promote his book - accompanied by Veronica and her mother, Ethel. Although Ali and Belinda were not yet divorced, Veronica was now travelling openly with him. Ali was captivated by her beauty and was unable to give her up to save his marriage, even though Belinda was an excellent wife and mother whom everybody admired. He refused to talk about his marital problems with newsmen, saying to them, 'You people are too intelligent to talk about my personal life.'

Opposite: Ali at Heathrow with the co-writer of *The Greatest*, Richard Durham, who was an editor for the Nation of Islam's newspaper, *Muhammad Speaks*. Ali and his entourage - this time of only nine people - were staying at the Carlton Tower Hotel in Knightsbridge. He was to spend a few days in England, autographing copies of his book for the UK publisher, Granada Publishing.

Ali's 'other wife'

Opposite: Ali was happy to talk about money to reporters, saying he hoped to earn US$26 million in 1976, to enable him to retire. He commented that he had just been offered £18,000 to do a television commercial in Britain, but didn't think he would have time to fit it in. He was no stranger to advertising, having already appeared in adverts for milk, a bedtime drink and garden games.

Right: Belinda had walked out after Veronica was referred to as 'Ali's other wife' in an article about Manila. Ali was foolish enough to give a Press conference after the story broke, in which he said, 'Anybody who worries about who's my wife, tell them, you don't worry who I sleep with and I won't worry who you sleep with. The only person I answer to is Belinda Ali, and I don't worry about her.' Although it did not yet show, Veronica was already pregnant with their first child, Hana, who was born in August 1976.

Below: Ali receives an award at a Press conference at the Savoy Hotel in London in March 1976, for the UK launch of *The Greatest*.

A busy schedule

The Press conference for the launch of the book at the Savoy was attended by a mixed audience of publishers, public relations people, feature writers and sports journalists. It was one of 26 engagements, mostly interviews, that he was booked to do in the three days he was in England.

Journalists were asked to restrict their questions to the book or Ali's life, but a few brave souls did bring up the subject of his troubled marriage. Ali again declined to answer, but was more communicative on the subject of his past opponents. He said of British boxer Brian London, whom he had fought ten years previously, 'He was a pretty good fighter for a couple of rounds - but he didn't take a punch too good.'

In his biography, Ali revealed that all his bragging and boasting was done intentionally, to move people to hate him so they would long to see him beaten - and would pay US$200-300 a seat to watch.

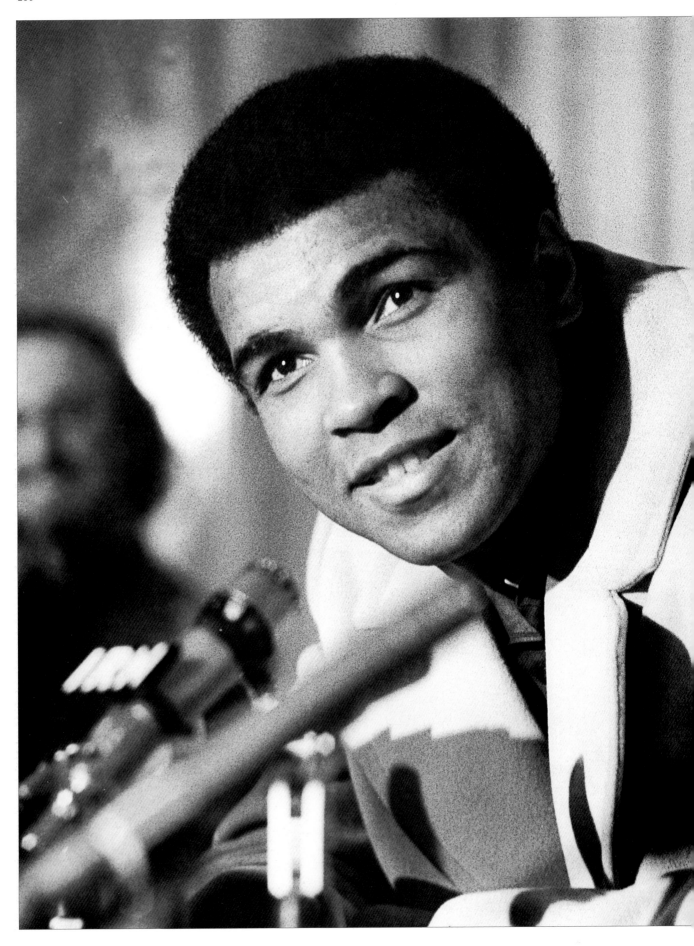

Out cold...

As well as the Press conference, Ali also gave several private interviews to selected journalists, while resting on a sofa in one of the Savoy's suites. Throughout his trip to England, he was suffering from a heavy cold and a cough, which had apparently plagued him for several weeks. He told reporters that his difficulty in shaking off the illness reminded him of his years. He was now 34, not old in real terms, but old for a professional boxer.

The Greatest was 413 pages long and became an instant best-seller. Ali said of his biography, 'There's a lot about me you didn't know.' According to one reviewer, it was 'a most revealing, gripping, upsetting and, yes, tender and honest book'.

Ali arriving at the Savoy, followed by Jeremiah Shabazz, who was one of his spiritual teachers, and his younger brother.

Opposite above: Returning to his hotel in London from a party given in Reading by the director of his forthcoming film, *The Greatest*, Ali leans forward in the car to shield Veronica - wearing her white fur coat - from the cameras. The woman in the background is Veronica's mother. The film was to start production later that year and was released the following year by Columbia Pictures.

Opposite below: At a book-signing in London, the venue is packed with people from all walks of life. Ali, as usual, had a smile and a word for nearly all of them.

Over-weight and out of shape

Right: After an easy fight against Belgian heavyweight champion Jean-Pierre Coopman in February 1976, Ali went into training again near Washington, preparing to fight Jimmy Young. Everyone expected it to be another easy bout, and since Ali now found training hard he tended to cut corners and went into the ring out of shape.

Below: The Ali-Young bout was the first title fight to be held in the Washington area for 35 years. For a challenger, Young was a pretty passive figure, and it fell to Ali to come up with some aggression at the weigh-in.

Opposite above: All the messing around distracted from the fact that at 230lbs - the heaviest of his boxing career - Ali was 21lbs heavier than Young.

Opposite below: The fight was a big disappointment to the audience, it was dull and boring and Ali was slow and showed none of his usual magic. He should have disposed of Young quickly, but it dragged on to the full fifteen rounds.

Just a circus...

Opposite: As a challenger for the world title, Young was expected to fight to win but he still couldn't come up with the required aggression. On several occasions, when he was caught by Ali, Young simply stuck his head through the ropes, bringing the bout to a halt. Even so, Ali's poor showing meant he was lucky to be awarded the win on points. Afterwards Dundee said, 'It was horrible, it was a nightmare… But I don't think Ali will take anyone so cheaply again. Frankly, I wish there were five more Joe Fraziers or George Foremans for him to fight, then I'd never have to worry about him keeping his mind on business.'

Above and right: Ali was determined that he would not let his public down again, and for his next fight, against England's Richard Dunn in Germany, he took his physical preparation very seriously. In Munich both fighters used the same 'gym' - a converted circus ring - for training, taking it in turns. Ali did a series of vigorous workouts, aimed at shedding the excess pounds he was carrying, watched by over 2,000 spectators.

'Dunn is going to get done!'

Right: While visiting Dunn to watch him sparring, Ali taunted him by calling him 'Frankenstein's monster'. The British and European champion ignored him and carried on training, watched by 1400 people who had paid £2 each to see him work out.

Below: Ali playfully tries to climb into the ring with Dunn and is stopped by his brother, on the left, and other members of his entourage. He left after about 20 minutes, shouting, 'Dunn is going to get done!'

Dunn retorted, 'Ali is talking well at the moment, but it will be a different story once the bell sounds for the first round. Then it will just be him and me.'

Opposite: During his trip to London in March, Ali had met Dunn in a gym that had been set up in Quaglino's in the West End. The confrontation was partly to boost ticket sales for Dunn's challenge for the vacant European title, against Bernd August of West Germany, which was to be held at the Albert Hall on April 6, and also to promote the Ali-Dunn bout.

Advice from the champ

Ali playfully squares up to Dunn. For the champ, the fight with Dunn would be one more in a long line of defences of his title, but for the challenger it was a rare chance to fight in the big league - and for a big purse.

A rare moment of public introspection, as Ali listens to Dunn speak. Dunn was a comparative newcomer to international boxing, and Ali gave him a few tips for his forthcoming fight with August, which Dunn went on to win.

Fighting fit

A week before the fight, Dunn suspended his training after his weight dropped 9lbs below the level he planned for the fight. He took the day off and drove to the mountains; he also planned to cut some of his early morning running and miss his Thursday training session in a bid to regain the weight. When Ali heard about it, he said, 'Dunn was smart. Joe Bugner was overtrained when he fought me and Jimmy Young too. It's happened to me and the best thing is just to lay off.'

Ali himself seemed so pleased with his training that he announced he wanted to meet the winner of the Frazier-Foreman bout. He was still over 220lbs, but expected to lose at least 3lbs before the fight.

Training for both fighters was completed on May 24. Dunn proclaimed confidently that he could upset Ali. 'I know I can do it, even if the rest of them don't give me a chance at all.'

Opposite: Before the fight in Munich.

Cost of tickets 'sinful'

Tickets for the Ali-Dunn fight had sold very poorly - partly because of the poor show at Ali's last fight. Also people in Munich were not interested in the fight and thought the seats were overpriced, with a local newspaper describing the cost as 'sinful'. On the eve of the fight, Ali took a cut in his purse in return for 2000 tickets, which he gave out to American military personnel stationed in Germany.

At the weigh-in, Ali was badly shaken when the stage collapsed, tumbling him and several others more than 6 feet onto wooden planking. Ali was not hurt, but Bundini suffered cuts to both legs. It happened shortly after Ali had been weighed at 220lbs; Dunn had already weighed-in at 206½lbs and left the stage.

The audience included many famous faces, including Prince Rainier and Princess Grace of Monaco, Candice Bergen, Burt Lancaster and Elizabeth Taylor.

A bid for control...

After the bell, Dunn came out with all the determination of a serious challenger for the title. A southpaw, he stood with his right foot forward, presenting an awkward target for a fighter like Ali - who at least had the speed to move into position for sharp right-hand counters.

For a while, Dunn was able to smack home some hard right jabs in front of Ali's left lead, because he went forward instead of trying to stay back and slip the champ's lightning jabs.

While Ali was preparing for the fight, promoter Don King was making a bid for control of his career. Herbert Muhammad was still Ali's manager, but since his father had died the previous year, Muhammad had spent quite a bit of time away from Ali, helping his brother to keep the community of the Nation of Islam together. King seized the opportunity offered by his absence, but had underestimated Ali's bond to Muhammad so the attempt eventually failed.

A question of survival

In the third round, Ali began to dance, raised the pace and improved his timing. He began to unravel Dunn's defence and bring out his best shots, bent on defeating someone to whom he could not lose. From the moment a blow from Ali's right hand sent the challenger to his knees, it was a question of survival for the British and European champion. Dunn was knocked to the floor three times in the fourth, but he refused to give in and just kept on coming.

In the fifth, Dunn was again floored twice by Ali, but nothing halted him. Finally the referee deliberately counted him out on his feet, awarding Ali a technical knock-out. The decision was even accepted by the Press - particularly the British, who did not want to see such a brave fighter end up with a serious injury.

A fiasco...

Ali said of Dunn afterwards, 'He gave me more trouble than I expected. He hit me real good a couple of times. I give him credit for a great match.' When Dunn returned to his hotel after the fight, those waiting in the lobby broke into applause. Dunn also earned praise from reporters for his courage. 'Dunn's determination to try and make a fight of it makes Bugner's showing against Ali look very sad.'

Opposite: Ali's next bout was a fiasco in more ways than one. He was booked to fight a champion Japanese wrestler, Antonio Inoki, at the Sudokan Hall in Japan. There were no fixed rules for such a fight, so a set was made up, with 15 three-minute rounds. The fight turned out to be very boring, because Inoki either grappled Ali or kicked to keep him at bay and the champ only managed to throw half a dozen punches, of which only two landed. On top of this, some of Inoki's kicks had caused severe damage to Ali's legs, and he had to be hospitalized later to repair the damage.

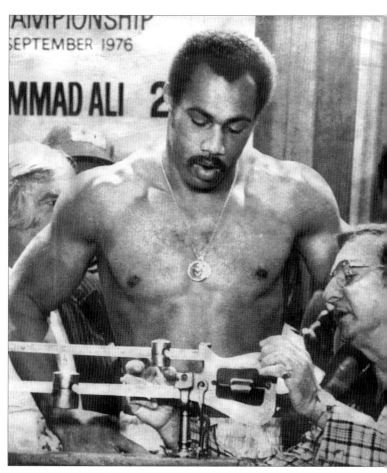

'I was robbed.'

Above left: Ken Norton puts his hand over Ali's mouth, as he steps up to address the National Press Club in Washington. Both fighters spoke to the gathering, which took place a month before their scheduled bout in September 1976.

Above: Norton weighs-in for the fight at 217½lbs, nearly 10lbs heavier than when he first fought Ali in March 1973. He explained the difference as being due to 'Father Time'.

Left: After Ali beat him, Norton said he was going to quit boxing. The bout had been so close it came down to the last round, which Norton felt had been unfairly awarded to Ali by the judges. 'I was robbed. I won ten rounds, at least nine.' He said later that he wasn't tired, and could have fought the last round all-out if his corner hadn't told him he had already won so not to take any chances.

Opposite: Annazette Chase playing Belinda Ali, alongside Ali playing himself, during filming of his first Hollywood film, *The Greatest*, in December 1976. A few members of the entourage appeared in the film themselves, but Ali and his second wife had filed for divorce three months previously.

'One of the worst fights ever fought'

Above: After Norton, it was over 7 months before Ali fought another championship bout, against Alfredo Evangelista of Spain. The crowd of 12,000 were mainly Ali fans, rather than boxing fans, and didn't really care how good the boxing was as long as their hero won. Evangelista was a poor fighter, but even his greatest fans acknowledged that Ali was past his best, so the fight was close.

Left: Evangelista and Ali square up. Afterwards, most sporting pundits agreed that the fight had been boring. but Howard Cosell, who covered the bout for ABC television went further; 'It was one of the worst fights ever fought.'

Opposite: Ali lands a deft jab. Despite Evangelista's inexperience, the fight went to fifteen rounds, before being awarded to Ali on a decision.

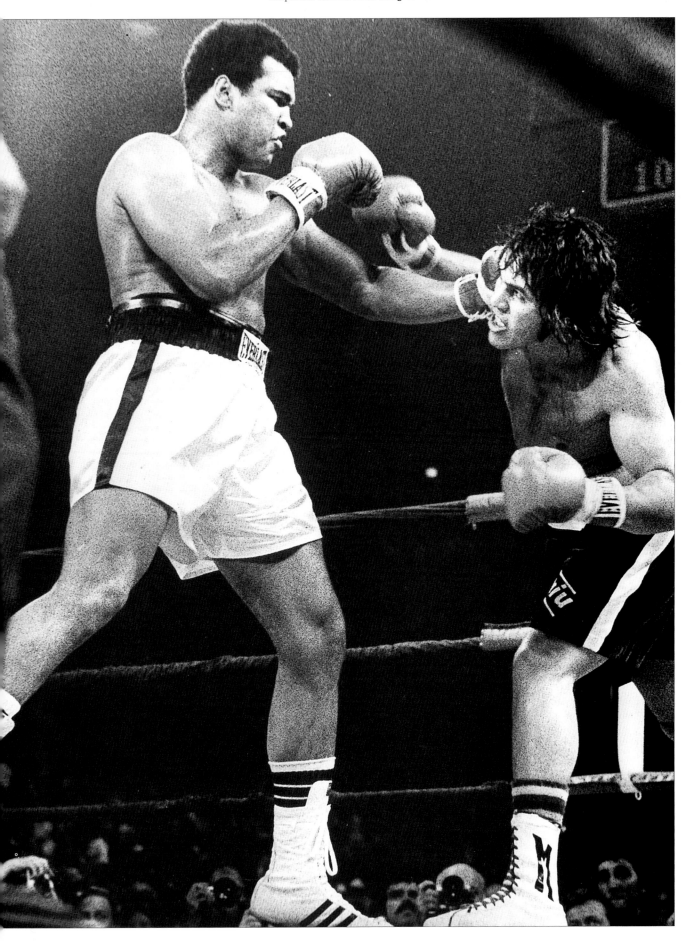

The greatest dad...

Above: In England in August 1977 to attend the UK premiere of his film *The Greatest*, Ali is a guest on the BBC Radio One show, *Open House*. Presenter Pete Murray takes it on the chin as Ali shoots a right.

Left: At the headquarters of London's Capital Radio, Ali is presented with his portrait by the artist, Selwood S Ballard of Bexley, Kent.

Opposite above: During a lunchtime Press conference at the Café Royal to promote his film, Ali's one-year-old daughter, Hana, bursts into noisy tears to get her share of the attention.

Opposite below: Ali, renowned for his speed in the boxing ring, is also quick off the mark with the feeding bottle, and peace is speedily restored. Ali was strangely reluctant to talk about the film, preferring to discuss love, peace and racial harmony instead.

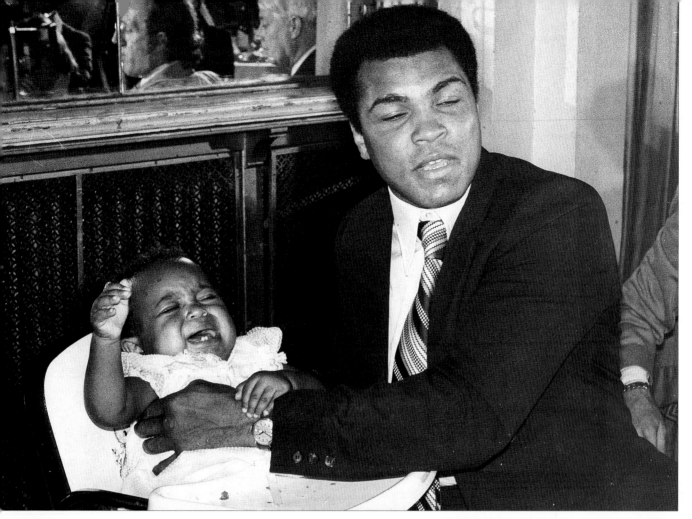

The champ loses a title...

Opposite: Ali displays an award at a reception in London given by the Victoria Sporting Club, at which he was guest of honour.

Below: Britain's international sprinter, Sonia Lannaman, is greeted with a kiss from Ali at the Victoria Sporting Club reception.

Right: The doting father carries Hana. She was a great hit with the British Press, who declared she had stolen her father's title and was now 'the prettiest'. Ali and Veronica had married only two months previously in Los Angeles, after which they had gone on a very short honeymoon to Hawaii.

Below right: As he arrives at Great Ormond Street Hospital for Sick Children, Ali is greeted by a happy and enthusiastic crowd of children and staff. He had come to present a Sunshine Coach for taking the children on outings, to the Dean of the Institute of Child Health, Professor JA Dudgeon. The coach had been sponsored to the tune of £5000 by Variety Club of Great Britain member Sidney Hillman and his family, with the balance being met by the Hospital Board and the Friends of the Hospital.

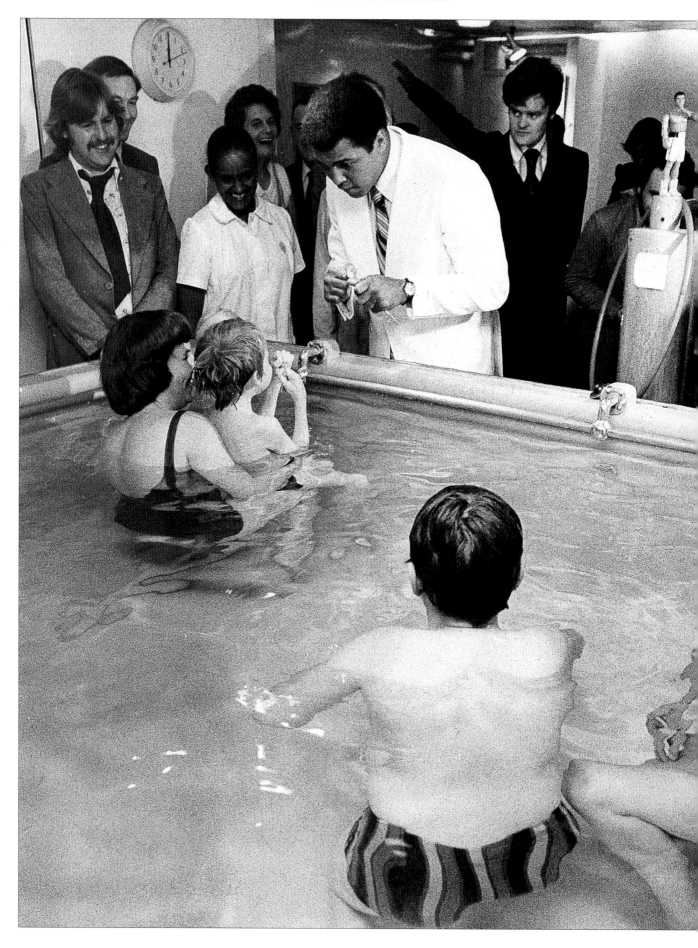

Standing out in the crowd...

Opposite: Ali demonstrates one of his magic tricks to eight-year-old Jason Baker and nurse Jan Hughes in the therapy pool, watched by ten-year-old Jonathan Hargood and some of the staff.

Above: The London premiere of *The Greatest* was held at The Empire, Leicester Square, and thousands of fans surrounded Ali as he arrived. Hysterical young girls pressed forward to catch a glimpse of the champ and one fainted in the crush and was taken to hospital with neck and head injuries. As well as Ali himself, the film also featured Ernest Borgnine, Robert Duvall and James Earl Jones.

Right: South Shields in the north of England turns out in thousands to welcome Ali, who had come on a three-day trip to help raise money for local boys' clubs. On the bus with him were several other boxers, including Richard Dunn, Dave Green, Terry Downes and Terry Spinks. The poster of the queen had been left on the bus after her visit the day before.

Salute from the champ

Opposite: Even handicapped by Hana, the champ manages a two-fisted salute to Press at Heathrow as he leaves Britain.

Despite the public brashness, Ali was much quieter in private. Many of his friends could vouch for his kindness and generosity, both to them and to strangers.

Chapter Eight

'This is my last fight'

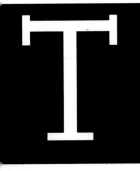hose around Ali were not blind to his condition, but they thought he could continue as champ if he only fought easy fights. It was a short-term strategy, because sooner or later some up-and-coming young blood was going to want his title - just as he had taken it from Sonny Liston all those years ago. Ali still had his skill and cunning to keep him on top, and perhaps more than any other boxer he had always been an instinctive fighter, able to take advantage of prevailing conditions and change tactics, rather than sticking to a set plan. He was still big and strong, and could summon up reserves of stamina when it was needed, but not so quickly or easily as he once had. He had also lost much of his astonishing speed in the ring - and perhaps more worrying, he now gloried in the punishment he could take, as once he had gloried in being too fast to hit. Mentally he still wanted to be champion, but he wasn't hungry for it as he had once been and didn't want to bother with the discipline of training any more.

Against this background, he was approached to fight Leon Spinks. Initially Ali said no, because Spinks was very inexperienced - he was an Olympic gold medal winner who had only fought five professional fights - but after seeing Spinks fight Scott LeDoux, he changed his mind. Spinks was only 24, a good street-fighter rather than a boxer, uneducated and something of a free spirit. He wasn't ranked in the top ten, so he had to fight an Italian, Alfio Righetti, to qualify for a bout against the world champion. No one expected him to beat Ali, and in many ways he was his own worst enemy, skipping out of training camp regularly to go to night clubs because he felt cooped up. What he did have was a burning desire to be someone, and his youth and strength went a long way to make up for his lack of boxing skill. Ali, on the other hand, started training more than 20lbs overweight and did less than 25 rounds of sparring in preparation. On the night, Ali did his 'rope-a-dope' for the early rounds, hoping Spinks would tire himself out punching. Unfortunately it was Ali himself who tired, while Spinks still had plenty of energy to stop the out-of-condition champion from fighting back in later rounds. Ali lost his title in the ring for the first time, and to a novice with limited skills; he could not walk away and let it rest like that.

Although Ali wanted a rematch against Spinks, the World Boxing Council ruled that Spinks should fight Ken Norton, and that if he went for a rematch with Ali instead they would strip him of his title. In this they were not motivated by protecting Ali's health, but had been influenced by Don King, who wanted Spinks to fight one of his boxers. By now, King controlled most of the other major fighters, including Norton, and this was his chance to have the world heavyweight champion in his stable. But Ali-Spinks was where the money was, so the rematch was agreed. The WBC duly took the title from Spinks and gave it to Norton, but the other ruling authority, the World Boxing Association, stayed with Spinks and again the title was split.

Ali went into serious training for his rematch with Spinks. He told Pat Putnam of *Sports Illustrated*, 'I've worked this hard for fights before, but never for this long. All the time I'm in pain... I hate it, but I know this is my last fight.' By the evening of the contest, he was in better shape than he had been for years. By contrast, Spinks had avoided training and spent much of his time as champion partying and smoking dope. Despite this, predictions about the result were cautious - Ali was still not nearly as good as he had been and Spinks was 12 years younger and a natural brawler. The bout was slow, but Ali avoided the ropes and stayed in control so the judges were unanimous in awarding him the fight.

Even though Ali had told *Sports Illustrated* beforehand that the fight with Spinks would be his last, he did not officially retire until nine months later. Meanwhile a whole host of crazy offers were made to try and tempt him back into the ring, but Ali was having none of it. 'Everybody grows old,' he told reporters. 'I'd be a fool to fight again.'

He still needed to earn money, however, particularly since his wife Veronica had expensive tastes, so he had become involved in a series of projects outside boxing. As well as another lecture tour, his name was licensed to promote Idaho potatoes, there was a ten-city farewell tour of Europe and he starred with Kris Kristofferson in a four-hour mini-series, *Freedom Road*. It was well received, but acting was never going to bring Ali the sort of money he had earned fighting. Unfortunately, not much of that was left.

During his career, Ali had earned many millions of dollars but his finances had not been well looked after. Apart from the bad deals he was talked into, there was also his ever-expanding entourage, many of whom were only too happy to help him spend his earnings. A few took it further, exploiting their association with him and even stealing - either taking things directly or making deals with the people doing business with Ali, so they received a cut of the profit. Ali himself was outstandingly generous - money meant little to him unless it could be used to relieve other people's suffering. Word quickly spread that he was a soft touch, so he was constantly a target for con men and they rarely went away empty-handed. Maybe much of this would not have mattered if proper financial planning had been in place to ensure that there was enough left when Ali quit boxing, but this was not done. Efforts were made late in his career to sort out Ali's finances, but they were unsuccessful in the long term.

Since Ali had retired from boxing, he no longer took the exercise he once had. His weight shot up to over 30lbs more than it was in his prime, and he began to look bloated and unfit. People had always commented on how beautiful he looked, and much of that was to do with the fact that his skin seemed to glow with energy when he was fit and healthy. Now it looked dull and lifeless and the first signs of the deterioration in his speech were becoming apparent. It would obviously have been madness for him to consider returning to boxing - but of course that is exactly what Ali decided to do.

Many explanations have been offered as to why Ali agreed to return to the ring, after two years of retirement. Maybe he needed the money, perhaps he did it because everyone told him not to, he may just have found he missed the action too much. He initially agreed to fight the WBA heavyweight title holder, John Tate, but the fight was postponed after Ali was punched in the mouth during training, causing a gash that needed stitches. While he was recuperating, Tate was defeated by Mike Weaver and although alternative opponents were considered, for various reasons they were not suitable. The current WBC heavyweight champion was Larry Holmes, who had taken the title off Ken Norton in 1978 only three months after it was awarded. Holmes had also beaten Weaver, so he began to seem like the logical choice for Ali.

Holmes was really reluctant to fight Ali and he told everyone that Ali shouldn't fight again, but when it came down to it he couldn't just turn the bout down. Ali went into training, but questions were raised over the state of his health. His old physician Ferdie Pacheco, said publicly that he shouldn't return to boxing an even his mother said she didn't want to see him in the ring again Finally Ali went into the respected Mayo Clinic for two days, to b checked out and given a medical certificate before the Nevada Stat Athletic Commission would grant him a licence to fight. For a ma of his age, Ali was in excellent health, but as a boxer he was not i such good condition. The report noted several problems that coul have been put down to neurological damage, but the commissio nevertheless gave Ali his licence. Then, just before the fight, a docto misdiagnosed Ali as having a hypothyroid condition - even thoug nothing of the sort had been mentioned in the Mayo Clinic repor - and prescribed drugs to bring it under control. Ali began to tak many more than the recommended dose, in the belief that thi would increase his energy. The drugs had the opposite effect making him lethargic, dehydrated and tired. Despite all this th fight went ahead. From the beginning it was obvious that Holme could hit Ali at will but the fight continued into the tenth round Finally Dundee signalled to the referee to stop the slaughter an instead of going out in a blaze of glory as he had planned, Ali wa going as a beaten man.

Right: Ali and Veronica both look subdued as they arrive in London en route to Bangladesh, just after he has lost his title to Leon Spinks. After his visit, he was appointed Honorary Consul General to the country.

Previous page: Ali carries two-year-old Hana, as they arrive in London for a two-day visit at the end of 1978.

To Russia with love

Right: Ali meets Soviet leader Leonid Brezhnev during a successful 12-day goodwill tour of Russia in June 1978. He endeared himself to Muscovites by jogging round Red Square and shaking hands with people queuing to visit Lenin's tomb.

Below: Ali relaxes with Veronica. He took his training for the second fight with Spinks very seriously, running 3-5 miles every morning and sparring more than he had in years.

Opposite above: Ali at his devotions in a Tashkent mosque. On his return to Moscow he fought three two-round exhibition matches, but he was clearly unfit, which did not bode well for the rematch with Spinks coming up in September.

Opposite below: The second fight against Spinks was sluggish; Ali was feeling his years but Spinks had not done any training. The judges awarded the fight to Ali on points, so he had his title back.

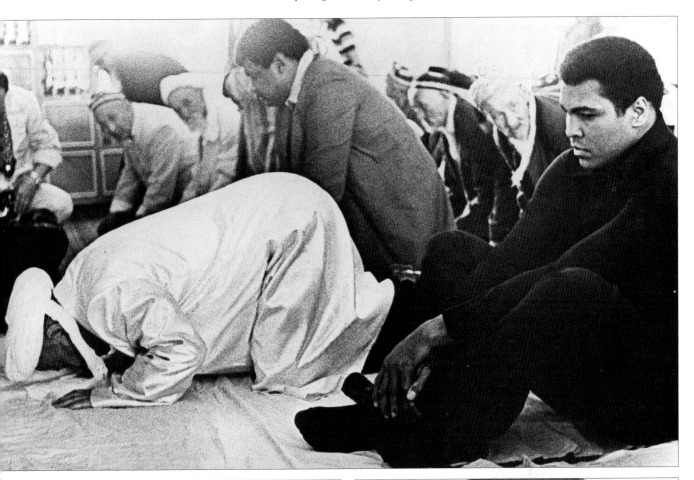

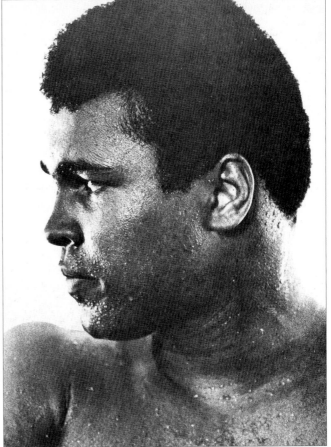

A bit of support from the champ

Opposite above: Ali at a Press conference, with promoters Butch Lewis of Top Rank, Dick Gregory and Don Hubbard of Louisiana Sports Inc. He was defending Lewis and Hubbard in their legal battle with the New Orleans promoters of the second Ali-Spinks fight.

Opposite below: At Grosvenor House in London, Ali cuddles his daughter Hana, while nine-month-old Laila makes a quick phone call. When she turned 21, Laila followed her father into the ring.

Above: The doting dad with Hana and Laila on their way back to America. They had been in England for two days, to record a television sports interview.

Right: In front of the Statue of Liberty, Ali lends his support to the leaders of the American Indian Movement in their protest against the conditions they are forced to live in after their lands were taken away.

A little help from my friends...

Right and below: British television personality Tom O'Connor helps Ali with his make-up for an appearance at the Rainbow Theatre in Finsbury Park, London, in January 1979. The show is a testimonial for former British heavyweight champion Joe Erskine, and Ali said he was appearing because they needed him and, 'It's part of my beliefs. I have to make up for the bad things I've done if I want to go to Heaven.'

Opposite above: O'Connor separates Ali and his old opponent Henry Cooper, as they pretend to square up before the show at the Rainbow. During his spot, Ali just stood up and talked to the audience - and they loved it.

Opposite below: In a few days Ali will celebrate his 37th birthday, so the children of Acton Green Middle School in London present him with a birthday cake.

'Happy Birthday, dear Ali!'

Right: Ali gets a birthday hug from fan Maureen White, as he leaves the Classic cinema in Haymarket, London.

Below: Before they presented the cake, the children had watched Ali starring in *Bangladesh I love You*, which had been filmed during his visit to the country the previous year.

Opposite above: Ali is almost mobbed by ground hostesses from Libyan Arab Airlines, when he flies into London from New York in May 1979. He was on his way to Tripoli, to fight a series of exhibition bouts.

Opposite below: Veronica looks on as Ali tells it like it is at a Press conference to publicize his European tour, which had been set up to generate some income now his career as a boxer was coming to an end. He had earned millions of dollars over the last few years, but little was left for his retirement.

Pleased to meet you...

Right: Ali with one of his paintings, several of which he donated to the UNICEF Year of the Child fund. The proceeds of an exhibition of his work in New York City also benefited the fund. He was always donating money or gifts to children who needed help.

Below: Veronica is never far from Ali's side as he travels round the world. Many members of his entourage are also still present - and some of them are continuing to use the opportunity to make money for themselves. Even when it became apparent that he had been taken advantage of, Ali was never willing to press charges. He always said that everybody made mistakes, and that the Lord wanted him to forgive. The upshot was that people did it again and again.

Opposite: A young fan greets the champ, as he arrives at the UK headquarters of Hertz, the car rental company, who are one of the sponsors of his European tour.

'I'm in the worst shape in the world'

Left: A very overweight butterfly surveys the world from the corner of the ring in May 1979. Ali was appearing in a demonstration bout in London, but now he was no longer in training, his weight had begun to shoot up. He told reporters, 'I'm in the worst shape in the world.'

Below: The punches no longer come with the speed of lightning, and his opponent has time to defend himself. The exhibition was held at the Royal Albert Hall, perhaps better known for musical evenings than as a fight venue.

Opposite above left: Having just completed a five-round exhibition bout with British heavyweight champion John L Gardener, Ali takes the microphone to tell the crowd that he expects to officially retire from boxing in about six weeks.

Opposite above right: One of his seconds helps Ali on with his robe. Unlike in proper fights, he wears a protector for exhibition bouts.

Opposite below: The expression says he's had enough - what is there left to fight for?

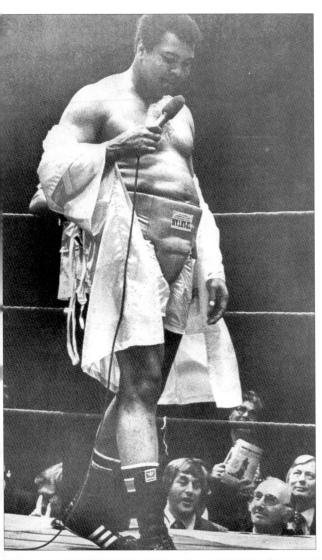

A star of stage and screen...

Right: Policeman Ray Egan presents the three-times world heavyweight champ with a commemorative plaque on behalf of the West Midlands Police Force, during a Press conference in Birmingham, England.

Below: Actress Joanna Lumley and actor Robert Powell with Ali at a party in his honour in June 1979.

Opposite above: British stars of stage and screen gather to bid goodbye to Ali, as he completes his European tour.

Opposite below: British sports writer Reg Gutteridge with Ali on *Muhammad Ali's Greatest Hits*, a show broadcast by Britain's ITV channel in 1979. Ali had also recently filmed a drama mini-series for American television with Kris Kristofferson called *Freedom Road*, in which he played an ex-slave who fought in the civil war and went on to become a United States senator.

Buy this car, or else...

After getting involved in a rather disastrous mission to Africa on behalf of President Carter, in which he tried to persuade the Africans to boycott the forthcoming Moscow Olympics because Russia had invaded Afghanistan, Ali left the world of diplomacy to promote Japanese cars. He announced at a Press conference in London in February 1980 that Toyota were paying him 'several million dollars' for radio and tv adverts aimed at the Saudi Arabian market.

Opposite above left: Ali poses with a Toyota Corolla.

Opposite above right: It may be a wine glass, but it contains a soft drink as Ali had never drunk alcohol.

Opposite below: Ali and John Conteh indulge in a spot of arm wrestling at the opening of Conteh's restaurant in London in 1980.

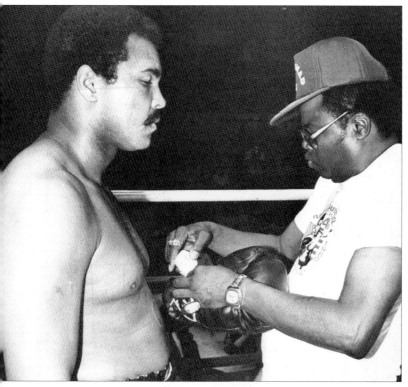

10 out of 10?

Opposite: Actress Bo Derek meets Ali as he begins training to fight the current world heavyweight champion, Larry Holmes, in October 1980. Holmes had been reluctant to fight Ali, but there was no way he could turn the bout down.

Left: Although he was very overweight and in spite of the issues that had been raised about his fitness, Ali was granted a licence to fight Holmes. He still had many of his instinctive skills, but his speed and agility were not as good as they were, his speech was already becoming slurred - and the drugs he was given for a supposed hypothyroid condition made things much worse.

Below: Most people close to Ali were against the fight, but it went ahead anyway. It was in many other people's interest that it should. For instance, Don King controlled Holmes, so after Ali was beaten by his man he was well on the way to achieving his ambition to control large parts of boxing and make a great deal of money.

The beginning of the end

Right: Ali takes time to give four-year-old Hana a cuddle, before the Holmes fight.

Below left: Despite still being overweight, Ali looked pretty good before the fight - but it was an illusion. All he had was his courage and his pride, which kept him on his feet despite the beating he was taking. At the end of round ten the fight was stopped and Holmes was declared the winner.

Below right: Two months later, Ali looks sad but fit as he arrives in London to promote *Freedom Road*, which is to have a Gala European Charity Premiere in London.

Opposite above: There was little sign of the outrageous performer of old as he moved through the crowds saying little, but kissing, shadow-boxing and leaving behind a trail of smiling faces.

Opposite below: Signing autographs for young fans on his way through Heathrow airport.

'I don't need boxing'

In his hotel after the Press conference for *Freedom Road*, Ali chats to a journalist from the British *Daily Mail* newspaper. He had been promising to return to boxing - although the experts were praying he would call it a day while the glory remained - but now it looked increasingly unlikely. 'I don't need boxing,' he said. 'What you thought you needed yesterday you are sometimes shown you don't need tomorrow.'

We meet again...

Right: Outside the Dorchester Hotel in London, Ali checks for rain - although he is well prepared for the changeable English weather.

Below: At the press reception at the Dorchester, Ali meets Tony Madigan again after twenty years. Madigan had been a joint bronze medallist when Ali won his gold at the Rome Olympics in 1960, and was now a journalist for *The Australian*.

Opposite above: Ali and a female journalist emerge laughing from the revolving doors of the Café Royal in London, after having inadvertently been caught in the same section.

Opposite below: Caught by a group of fans outside the House of Commons in London, Ali is happy to sign autographs. He was on his way to visit British politician Martin Stevens, MP.

Ali always had time for people - particularly children. As he and Veronica leave London for America, a young girl just looking for an autograph catches his full attention.

Chapter Nine

'We all grow old'

After the disastrous fight with Holmes, some of his entourage were quick to tell Ali that the medication he had been taking was the sole reason for his defeat, and that once everything was back to normal he would be able to box again. He was not hard to persuade - he wanted to finish his career fighting, not collapsed in his corner. In the meantime, he busied himself with his commercial projects, as well as doing television interviews and becoming involved in more charity work. He stopped taking all the medication that had been wrongly prescribed and tried hard to regain his former good health.

Unfortunately, he soon had another major problem to worry about. Early in 1981, it became evident that Ali's name had been used to defraud over $21 million from the Wells Fargo Bank in California. Some years ago, Ali had met Harold Smith, who later became involved in amateur boxing and formed the Muhammad Ali Amateur Boxing Team. He then suggested to Ali that they should form an organization to protect the fighters when they turned professional, and Muhammad Ali Professional Sports was started up. For the use of his name, Ali was to receive 25% of the profits from events, plus appearance fees for various promotions. Smith proceeded to promote fights - but he also began to embezzle funds from the Wells Fargo Bank in conjunction with a bank employee called Ben Lewis. Ali was totally unaware of what had been going on, but his name had been used as bait to convince the bank to open a line of credit and to get Lewis involved in the scam. When the scandal broke, Ali held a Press conference at which he told reporters, 'A guy used my name to embezzle $21 million. Ain't many names that can steal that much.' No one seriously suggested that Ali was in any way responsible, but his name had been tarnished and devalued - which was to affect his earnings after he retired from boxing.

However, while all this was going on, Ali was not planning a graceful retirement but aiming to have one more go at fighting, against Trevor Berbick at the end of the following year. It was difficult to arouse interest in the bout - none of the closed-circuit TV companies wanted to be involved, the major national networks refused to bid and many of the regular writers decided not to attend. Even though Don King was not directly involved in the promotion he tried to cut himself a piece of the action, since he had an option on Berbick's fights. Few people had ever stood up to him, but this time he provoked one of the Nation of Islam members putting the promotion together and was attacked and badly beaten up by his bodyguards.

Ali looked terrible in training and often walked rather than ran when doing his roadwork. He was 39 years old and his weight was up to 236lbs; he had no chance of winning against a young, fit boxer. He was being told by everyone not to fight, but he said, 'People need challenges. What's wrong with me trying to win the title a fourth time?' As for the fight itself, it was a shambles - the promoters lost the key to the gate, so it started two hours late, there were only two pairs of gloves so they had to be unlaced between each fight instead of cut off, and the bell was a cow bell. It was a poor ending for someone who had fought with such professionalism throughout his career - and of course Ali lost.

This time even he accepted the inevitable. He told a Press conference afterwards, '…I know it's the end; I'm not crazy … but at least I didn't go down. We all lose sometimes. We all grow old.' He had fought 61 professional fights in his career, of which he had won all but five. He had been unable to fight for three and a half years during his prime as a result of his legal problems with the draft board, but had still won the world heavyweight title three times. He deserved a peaceful retirement, but things didn't quite turn out that way.

First of all, in 1984, he was diagnosed as suffering from Parkinson's Syndrome, a neurological problem that had been brought on by damaged brain cells from blows to the head during his boxing career. Unlike Parkinson's disease, in which brain cells continue to degenerate and die, Parkinson's Syndrome is not progressive, so it was initially thought that with medication Ali could lead a mostly normal life. Unfortunately Ali had never been good with medication, and often refused to take his pills regularly. Without boxing, he had lost the means of defining his life, and for a while he drifted with little purpose. Meanwhile his third marriage was in trouble and by 1986 he and Veronica were divorced - with Veronica taking a large share of the money. However, since the early 1980s Lonnie Williams, who had known and loved Ali since she was a child, had lived nearby and tried to do what she could to look after him. Their friendship was very close and after the divorce he asked her to marry him. Their marriage remained strong and Lonnie not only loved and cared for him; as a graduate from business school, she was also very well-placed to manage his business interests.

Ali could have gradually disappeared from public sight after his retirement, particularly in view of his health problems. These were perhaps not as bad as they have sometimes been reported, although the diagnosis has since been revised, and it now appears certain that he has Parkinson's disease, which is slowly getting worse. Ali himself has accepted this as Allah's will, and perhaps uses his illness to protect himself from the world. 'I'm just a man like everyone else. People think I'm suffering, but I ain't suffering. If I didn't have this health problem, I'd be talking like I used to, trying to keep up with my image, doing all these interviews and commercials and speeches. I'd probably have a miserable life. I wouldn't be human.' He does not always speak clearly and has difficulty co-ordinating his movements, but his mind is sharp and his memory is good. He is still a mischievous practical joker and likes performing magic tricks for children. He spends a great deal of time at home studying the Islamic faith, reading the Qur'an and signing Islamic tracts to spread his beliefs, but his life is anything but quiet. He travels a great deal, and wherever he goes is still recognized and mobbed for his autograph. He tries to use his fame for public good as much as possible - he visits American schools to promote racial healing and in February 1985 he travelled to Beirut to try and negotiate the release of four American diplomats. In 1990 he went to Iraq to try to forestall the war; he was not successful, but he did manage to return with 15 of the American hostages who were being used as part of Saddam Hussein's 'human shield'. He has always been very generous with his time as well as his money and his door is forever open to strangers as well as to friends. Unfortunately this also means that people can still easily take advantage of his good nature

and forgiveness. But above all, he is happy and enjoys life.

In 1996, Ali was chosen to light the Olympic flame to start the games in Atlanta. The world watched as he walked to the top of the stadium carrying the Olympic torch, and it brought him back into the public eye. Now there are plans to build a Muhammad Ali Center in his hometown of Louisville, which will be partly a museum to document and celebrate his career as a boxer and partly an effort to reach out to young people and promote racial understanding and harmony. After he retired from boxing, many people began to look for another Muhammad Ali to replace him - but they will be disappointed. He was always more than just a famous sportsman - he is a man who stood firm for something he believed in, despite the personal cost, and who continues to try and do good in the world. As he once said himself, 'You won't see another like me for 200 years.'

Ali giving a dazzling display of conjuring in his hotel suite.

Right: Ali might not have perfect health these days, but he has a very full life, travelling round the world for charitable causes.

Previous page: Arriving in Britain from Los Angeles in August 1983, Ali looks calm and relaxed after the long flight - even though he still feared flying.

'Louisville Lip' meets the 'Mersey Mouth'

Above: A confrontation between the Louisiana Lip and the Mersey Mouth, when Ali appears with Freddie Starr on the Parkinson Show on Britain's BBC1 television channel. After making the introduction, Parkinson sat back and let the cameras roll as the verbal sparring match between his two guests went on for 2 hours. Edited highlights were transmitted on January 17, 1981.

Right: A lucky autograph hunter manages to get Ali's signature on his visit to London, during which he told reporters, 'I'm finished with boxing now. I'm going to enjoy the money I've made.'

Opposite: When he took his medication, Ali appeared back on form just like the old days, smiling and waving and full of jokes for anyone who would listen. When he refused to take his pills or forgot, he looked and moved like an old man, and his voice became slurred and difficult to understand.

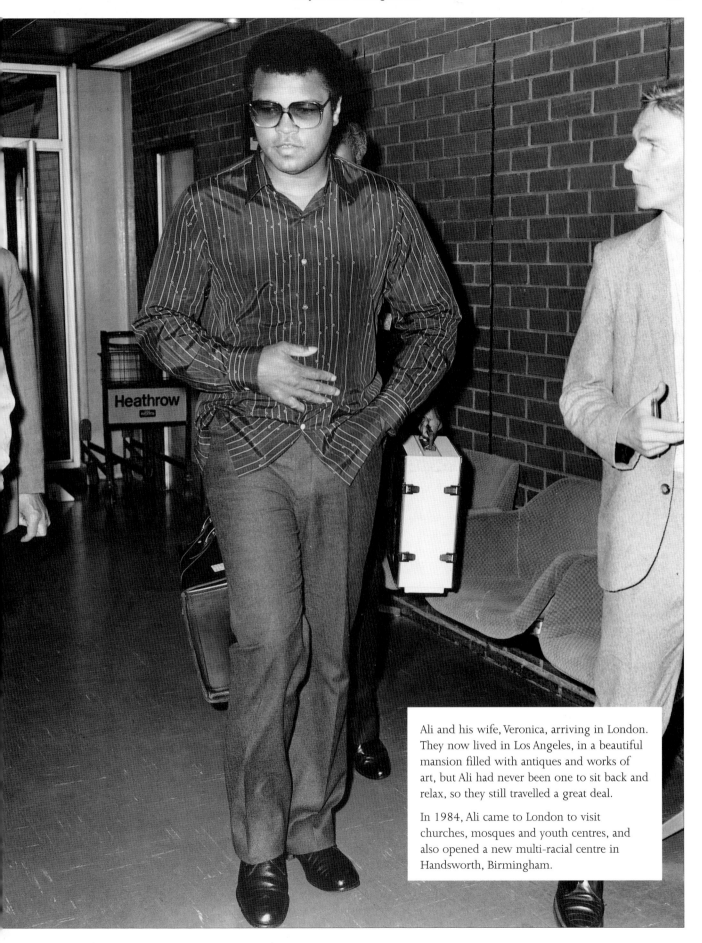

Ali and his wife, Veronica, arriving in London. They now lived in Los Angeles, in a beautiful mansion filled with antiques and works of art, but Ali had never been one to sit back and relax, so they still travelled a great deal.

In 1984, Ali came to London to visit churches, mosques and youth centres, and also opened a new multi-racial centre in Handsworth, Birmingham.

Back on form...

Right above: Ali addresses those attending a service in Birmingham's Grand Mosque.

Right centre: Sitting on the floor at Birmingham's Grand Mosque, Ali listens intently to the Imam.

Below: Ali pretends to stage a hold-up during a surprise visit to a branch of Barclays Bank in Birmingham. He was in the city to open a multi-racial cultural centre to be named after him, but he arrived two hours late and the crowd became very restive. The event degenerated into a fracas between 100 youngsters, police and officials at the centre, which left Ali unhurt but shaken.

Right below and opposite: Ali is back on top form when he returns the England in 1984. During his visit the previous year, Ali had appeared in very bad health and the newspapers were full of theories about brain damage.

That old black magic...

Right: Ali opens the Ideal Home Exhibition in Manchester and is then escorted round by security officers to help him when he has difficulty walking.

Below and opposite: In his hotel suite, Ali gives a dazzling, hour-long demonstration of magic to a group of reporters. He makes one handkerchief disappear, turns another into a walking stick and two coloured balls become one. The journalists are visibly impressed at his skill - but the British Magical Society are not. They announce they have stripped Ali of his honorary membership, for showing on daytime television how his tricks are done. Ali is unconcerned. 'I love doing magic for children, but I always show how I've tricked them so they can learn how easy it is to be deceived. I follow the religion of Islam, which preaches against deceit.'

Have book, will travel

During his constant travelling, Ali relaxes by reading the Qur'an or studying his books on prayer and Islam. Fellow passengers always recognise him, and they often come and ask after his health.

Ali's health is cause for concern

Left: In 1984, Ali's friends became increasingly concerned about his health and in September he checked into the Columbia-Presbyterian Medical Center in New York for tests. Afterwards, a Press statement was issued saying that he was suffering from Parkinson's Syndrome, not Parkinson's Disease. Parkinson's Disease is progressive, but the Syndrome is not, so there was every expectation that medication would stabilize his condition and allow him to live a normal life.

Below: Ali is carefully inspected by a young fan at New York airport.

Opposite above: A thoughtful Ali considers the doctor's verdict. It was apparent that he would need someone to care for him over the next few years, and make sure he took his medicine regularly for it to have the desired effect.

Opposite below: As usual, the Qur'an offers solace in times of trouble.

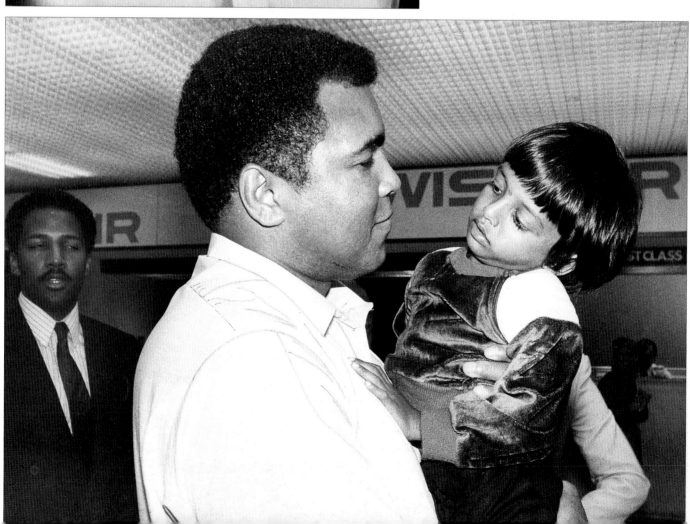

Money worries...

Right: It was not only Ali's health that was causing concern. Now he was no longer boxing, he was not earning nearly as much as he had been. The tens of millions of dollars that he had made during his twenty-year professional career had all but vanished, given away by Ali or frittered and stolen by some of the more unscrupulous members of the entourage.

Opposite: Attempts had been made to sort out his finances towards the end of his career and for a while they were successful. Then they began to founder, as the hangers-on began to talk Ali into going with their dubious schemes again, instead of those put forward by his professional financial advisors.

Below: Ali speaks to the Press in 1984, soon after coming out of the Columbia-Presbyterian Medical Center. The statement about his health had caused much of the wild speculation about him being 'punch-drunk' to die down.

'The Greatest' meets 'The Champ'

Promoter Don King and Ali arriving in England for the title fight between world heavyweight champion Tim Witherspoon and Britain's Frank Bruno in July 1986.

Opposite: Ali chats with Witherspoon in his training camp in Basildon, Essex. There were rumours that Ali had been joining the champ in his roadwork and intended trying to make yet another comeback.

A new life...

Ali arrives in London in October 1989 to promote a new video, *Champions Forever*.

Opposite: After his divorce from Veronica in 1986, Ali married Lonnie Williams, whom he had known since she was a child. She not only took care of his health, but also used her business training to try to sort out his finances.

Champions Forever

Old opponents Joe Frazier and George Foreman join Ali in the ring again - but this time not to fight. They have come together to promote the video, *Champions Forever*. The cleverly assembled film uses clips from Ali's most famous fights and shows him at the peak of his career.

Foreman had long ago reconciled his feelings about being beaten by Ali, and had once said, 'I realized I had lost to a great champion who transcended the sport of boxing, and that I should be proud to have been a big chapter in his legendary career.'

Despite the smiles, Frazier did not feel the same way. He never forgave Ali for some of the things said in the run-up to their fights, making fun of his intellect and calling him a gorilla. 'I don't like him but I got to say, in the ring he was a man. In Manila, I hit him punches... they'd have knocked a building down. He shook me in Manila; he won. But I sent him home worse than he came. Look at him now; he's damaged goods. He's finished, and I'm still here.'

Of his old foe, Ali said, 'I'm sorry Joe Frazier is mad at me. I'm sorry I hurt him; Joe Frazier is a good man'.

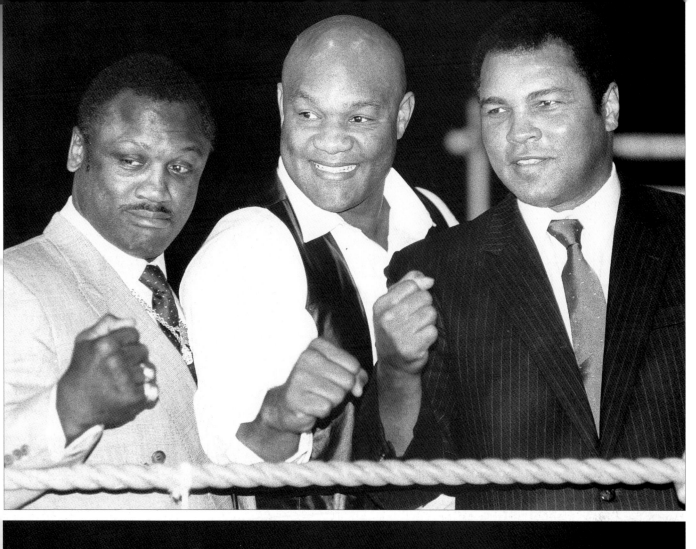

Still in the public eye

It is almost ten years since the last disastrous fight with Trevor Berbick, but Ali is still in the public eye and a new book about his life and career has recently been published.

Opposite: Ali at the London Docklands Arena, in October 1989.

Just like the old days

Henry Cooper joins Ali at the UK launch of *Muhammad Ali: His Life and Times*, by Thomas Hauser.

Opposite above: At a book-signing, crowds flock round Ali again - just like in the old days.

Opposite below: Arriving at St Bartholomew's Hospital in London to visit boxer Michael Watson, Ali stops to cuddle four-year-old Lucy Grant, who is suffering from leukemia; she had called to him as he walked past.

Get well soon

Ali and his twin daughters, Rasheeda and Jamillah, with Michael Watson's mother Joan outside the St Bartholomew's Hospital. Watson had suffered brain injuries during a fight against Chris Eubank, and Ali had asked if he could visit. He spent half an hour with Watson, joking and pretending to spar and the visit gave the injured fighter a huge boost.

As much lip as Ali

Ali with Geoffrey C Ewing, who played
the former champ in *Ali*, a one-man show,
which encapsulated Ali's life in two hours.
The play was staged at the Mermaid
Theatre in London in June 1993.

Opposite: Henry Cooper comes face-to-face
with his old opponent in the Mermaid
Theatre, at a special charity performance
of the play.

Best friends

Ali arrives back in London in November 1993 with one of his closest friends, photographer Howard Bingham. They had first met in April 1962, and Ali once said of him, 'Everybody says I love people, so it's only fair that I have the best friend in the world, and that's Howard Bingham. He never asks for anything; he's always there when someone needs him.'

Opposite below: Bingham and Ali greet Henry Cooper at his Old Kent Road gym in London, where Ali had popped in to meet the aspiring champions of the future.

A 30-year journey...

Above: Ali tries out Cooper's ring for size. He was in London to promote another book, *Muhammad Ali: A 30 Year Journey*.

Below: Dr Keith Smedi, Ali and Mike Tyson, pictured during one of Ali's visits to Britain.

Opposite: Ali rides in a vintage car, escorted by mounted policeman through the massive crowds, during a visit to Brixton in South London in 1999. After a few years out of the news, he had come back to prominence after lighting the Olympic flame at the Atlanta Games in 1996.

'I'm just getting started'

Stopping the car, Ali reaches out to shake hands with everyone he can reach and signs as many autographs as possible. In a recent interview he had said, 'People say I had a full life, but I ain't dead yet. I'm just getting started. Fighting injustice, fighting racism, fighting crime, fighting illiteracy, fighting poverty, using this face the world knows so well and going out and fighting for truth and different causes.'

Great sportsmen

Ali with Manchester United footballer David Beckham, at the BBC 'Sports Personality of the Year' awards ceremony in London in December 1999.

A night at the Savoy

Ali looks a touch concerned about the weather as he leaves the 'Sports Personality of the Year' awards ceremony.

Opposite: At a charity function hosted by Britain's *Daily Mail* newspaper at the London Savoy's River Room, Ali is happy to sign his autograph for fans.

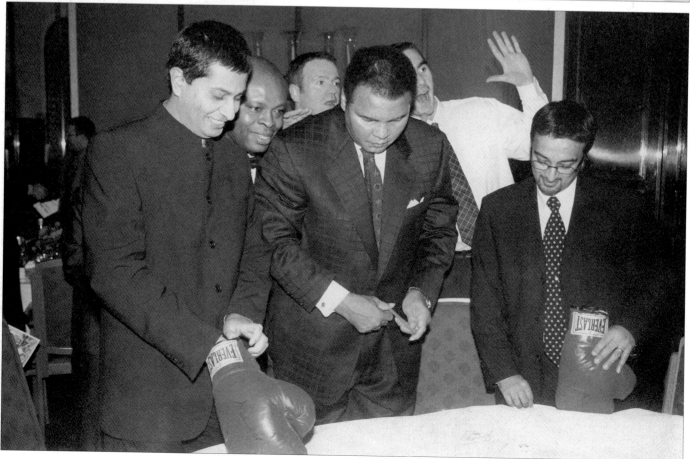

'A very special gift'

The day after being crowned sportsman of the year, Ali was guest of honour at a *Daily Mail* fundraising event in aid of prostate cancer research. The evening raised £100,000. Readers went on to contribute £1 million to the appeal.

Opposite: Most superstars last a few years, then for one reason or another their popularity begins to fade. Ali goes on and on, still one of the most recognizable men in the world. Despite his physical problems, he is happy with his life and continues to do everything in his power to make the world a better place. Someone once said of him, 'He was a very special gift for us all.'

Below: Ali with Ian Wooldridge.

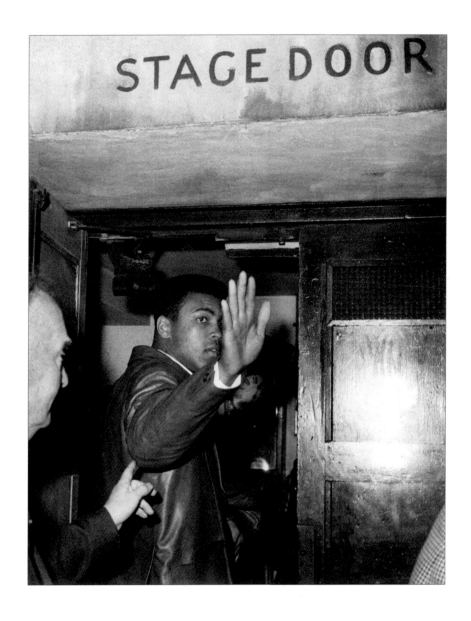

Professional Fight Chronology

1960

| 29 Oct | Tunney Hunsaker | Freedom Hall, Louisville, Kentucky | Win R6 |
| 27 Dec | Herb Siler | Auditorium, Miami Beach, Florida | KO R4 |

1961

17 Jan	Tony Esperti	Auditorium, Miami Beach, Florida	KO R3
07 Feb	Jim Robinson	Convention Hall, Miami Beach, Florida	KO R1
21 Feb	Donnie Fleeman	Convention Hall, Miami Beach, Florida	KO R7
19 Apr	Lamar Clark	Freedom Hall, Louisville, Kentucky	KO R2
26 Jun	Duke Sabedong	Convention Center, Las Vegas, Nevada	Win R10
22 Jul	Alonzo Johnson	Freedom Hall, Louisville, Kentucky	Win R10
07 Oct	Alex Miteff	Freedom Hall, Louisville, Kentucky	KO R6
29 Nov	Willi Besmanoff	Freedom Hall, Louisville, Kentucky	KO R7

1962

19 Feb	Sonny Banks	Madison Square Garden, New York City	KO R4
28 Mar	Don Warner	Convention Hall, Miami Beach, Florida	KO R4
23 Apr	George Logan	Memorial Sports Arena, Los Angeles	KO R6
19 May	Billy Daniels	St Nicholas Arena, New York City	KO R7
20 Jul	Alejandro Lavorante	Memorial Sports Arena, Los Angeles	KO R5
15 Nov	Archie Moore	Memorial Sports Arena, Los Angeles	KO R4

1963

24 Jan	Charlie Powell	Civic Arena, Pittsburgh, Pennsylvania	KO R3
13 Mar	Doug Jones	Madison Square Garden, New York City	Win R10
18 Jun	Henry Cooper	Wembley Stadium, London, England	KO R5

1964

| 25 Feb | Sonny Liston | Convention Hall, Miami Beach, Florida | (Wins World Heavyweight Title) KO R7 |

1965

25 May	Sonny Liston	St Dominic's Arena, Lewiston, ME	(Retains World Heavyweight Title) KO R1
31 Jul	Jimmy Ellis	San Juan, PR	Exhibition R3
31 Jul	Cody Jones	San Juan, PR	Exhibition R3
16 Aug	Cody Jones	Goteborg, Sweden	Exhibition R2

16 Aug	Jimmy Ellis	Goteborg, Sweden		Exhibition R2
20 Aug	Jimmy Ellis	London, England		Exhibition R4
20 Aug	Cody Jones	Paisley, Scotland		Exhibition R4
22 Nov	Floyd Patterson	Convention Center, Las Vegas	(Retains World Heavyweight Title)	KO R12

1966

29 Mar	George Chuvalo	Maple Leaf Gardens, Toronto, Canada	(Retains World Heavyweight Title)	Win R15
21 May	Henry Cooper	Highbury Stadium, London, England	(Retains World Heavyweight Title)	KO6
06 Aug	Brian London	Earls Court Stadium, London, England	(Retains World Heavyweight Title)	KO3
10 Sep	Karl Mildenberger	Wald Stadium, Frankfurt, Germany	(Retains World Heavyweight Title)	KO12
14 Nov	Cleveland Williams	Astrodome, Houston, Texas	(Retains World Heavyweight Title)	KO R3

1967

06 Feb	Ernie Terrell	Astrodome, Houston, Texas	(Retains World Heavyweight Title)	Win R15
22 Mar	Zora Folley	Madison Square Garden, New York City	(Retains World Heavyweight Title)	KO R7
15 Jun	Alvin Lewis	Detroit, Michigan		Exhibition R3
15 Jun	Orvill Qualls	Detroit, Michigan		Exhibition R3

1970

Sep	3 opponents	Morehouse College, Atlanta, Georgia		Exhibition
26 Oct	Jerry Quarry	Municipal Auditorium, Atlanta, Georgia		KO R3
07 Dec	Oscar Bonavena	Madison Square Garden, New York City		KO R15

1971

08 Mar	Joe Frazier	Madison Square Garden, New York City	(For World Heavyweight Title)	Lost R15
25 Jun	J.D. McCauley	Dayton, Ohio		Exhibition R2
25 Jun	Eddie Brooks	Dayton, Ohio		Exhibition R3
25 Jun	Rufus Brassell	Dayton, Ohio		Exhibition R3
30 Jun	Alex Mack	Charleston, SC		Exhibition R3
30 Jun	Eddie Brooks	Charleston, SC		Exhibition R4
26 Jul	Jimmy Ellis	Astrodome, Houston, Texas		KO R12
21 Aug	Lancer Johnson	Caracas		Exhibition R4
21 Aug	Eddie Brooks	Caracas		Exhibition R4
23 Aug	Lancer Johnson	Port of Spain		Exhibition R4
23 Aug	Eddie Brooks	Port of Spain		Exhibition R2
06 Nov	James Summerville	Buenos Aires		Exhibition R5
06 Nov	Miguel Paez	Buenos Aires		Exhibition R5
17 Nov	Buster Mathis	Astrodome, Houston, Texas		Win R12
26 Dec	Jürgen Blin	Hallenstadion Arena, Zurich, Switzerland		KO R7

1972

01 Apr	Mac Foster	Martial Arts Hall, Tokyo, Japan	Win R15
01 May	George Chuvalo	Pacific Coliseum, Vancouver, Canada	Win R12
27 Jun	Jerry Quarry	Convention Center, Las Vegas, Nevada	KO R7
01 Jul	Lonnie Bennett	Los Angeles, California	Exhibition R2
01 Jul	Eddie Jones	Los Angeles, California	Exhibition R2
01 Jul	Billy Ryan	Los Angeles, California	Exhibition R2
01 Jul	Charley James	Los Angeles, California	Exhibition R2
01 Jul	Rudy Clay	Los Angeles, California	Exhibition R2
19 Jul	Al Lewis	Croke Park, Dublin, Ireland	KO R11
24 Aug	Obie English	Baltimore, MD	Exhibition R4
24 Aug	Ray Anderson	Baltimore, MD	Exhibition R2
24 Aug	Alonzo Johnson	Baltimore, MD	Exhibition R2
24 Aug	George Hill	Baltimore, MD	Exhibition R2
28 Aug	Alonzo Johnson	Cleveland, Ohio	Exhibition R2
28 Aug	Amos Johnson	Cleveland, Ohio	Exhibition R2
28 Aug	Terry Daniels	Cleveland, Ohio	Exhibition R2
20 Sep	Floyd Patterson	Madison Square Garden, New York City	KO R7
11 Oct	John Dennis	Boston, Massachusetts	Exhibition R2
11 Oct	Cliff McDonald	Boston, Massachusetts	Exhibition R2
11 Oct	Doug Kirk	Boston, Massachusetts	Exhibition R2
11 Oct	Ray Anderson	Boston, Massachusetts	Exhibition R2
11 Oct	Paul Raymond	Boston, Massachusetts	Exhibition R2
21 Nov	Bob Foster	High Sierra Theater, Stateline, Nevada	KO R8

1973

14 Feb	Joe Bugner	Convention Center, Las Vegas, Nevada	Win R12
31 Mar	Ken Norton	Sports Arena, San Diego, California	Lost R12
10 Sep	Ken Norton	Forum, Inglewood, California	Win R12
20 Oct	Rudi Lubbers	Senyan Stadium, Jakarta, Indonesia	Win R12

1974

28 Jan	Joe Frazier	Madison Square Garden, New York City	Win R12
30 Oct	George Foreman	20th May Stadium, Kinshasa, Zaire	(Wins World Heavyweight Title) KO R8

1975

24 Mar	Chuck Wepner	Coliseum, Cleveland, Ohio	(Retains World Heavyweight Title) KO R15
16 May	Ron Lyle	Convention Center, Las Vegas, Nevada	(Retains World Heavyweight Title) KO R11

30 Jun	Joe Bugner	Merdeka Stadium, Kuala Lumpur, Malaysia	(Retains World Heavyweight Title) Win R15
01 Oct	Joe Frazier	Araheta Coliseum, Manila	(Retains World Heavyweight Title) KO R14

1976

20 Feb	Jean-Pierre Coopman	Clemente Coliseum, San Juan, Puerto Rico	(Retains World Heavyweight Title) KO R5
30 Apr	Jimmy Young	Capital Center, Landover, Maryland	(Retains World Heavyweight Title) Win R15
24 May	Richard Dunn	Olympiahalle, Munich, Germany	(Retains World Heavyweight Title) KO R5
25 Jun	Antonio Inoki	Tokyo, Japan	Exhibition D15
28 Sep	Ken Norton	Yankee Stadium, New York City	(Retains World Heavyweight Title) Win R15

1977

29 Jan	Peter Fuller	Boston, Massachusetts	Exhibition R4
29 Jan	Walter Haines	Boston, Massachusetts	Exhibition R1
29 Jan	Jerry Houston	Boston, Massachusetts	Exhibition R2
29 Jan	Ron Drinkwater	Boston, Massachusetts	Exhibition R2
29 Jan	Matt Ross	Boston, Massachusetts	Exhibition R2
29 Jan	Frank Smith	Boston, Massachusetts	Exhibition R1
16 May	Alfredo Evangelista	Capital Center, Landover, Maryland	(Retains World Heavyweight Title) Win R15
29 Sep	Earnie Shavers	Madison Square Garden, New York City	(Retains World Heavyweight Title) Win R15
02 Dec	Scott LeDoux	Chicago, Illinois	Exhibition R5

1978

15 Feb	Leon Spinks	Las Vegas Hilton, Las Vegas, Nevada	(Lost World Heavyweight Title) Lost R15
15 Sep	Leon Spinks	Superdome, New Orleans, Louisiana	(Won World Heavyweight Title) Win R15

1980

02 Oct	Larry Holmes	Caesar's Palace, Las Vegas, Nevada	(For World Heavyweight Title) Lost R11

1981

11 Dec	Trevor Berbick	QEII Sports Centre, Nassau, Bahamas	Lost R10

Event Chronology

1942

Jan 17   Cassius Marcellus Clay Jnr is born in Louisville General Hospital, in Kentucky

1954

Oct   Clay has his bike stolen at the Louisville Home Show and reports it to Joe Martin. Martin encourages him to learn to box

1960

Apr 18   Clay is registered for military draft

Aug   Clay represents the USA in the Boxing at the Rome Olympic Games and wins a gold medal

Oct 26   The gold medallist signs a managerial contract with the Louisville Sponsoring Group

Nov   Clay begins training with Archie Moore in California

Dec   After leaving Archie Moore's training camp, Clay returns home to Louisville

Dec 19   Clay begins training with Angelo Dundee in Miami

1961

Mar   Clay meets a member of the Nation of Islam who invites him to a meeting. He soon begins attending regularly

1962

Mar 9   Clay is classified 1-A, available for draft

Apr   Howard Bingham meets Clay in Los Angeles

Clay meets Malcolm X in Detroit

1963

Jan   Howard Bingham comes to Miami to stay with Clay for a while; it is the beginning of a lasting friendship

Mar   Drew Brown, better known as Bundini, meets Clay for the first time and joins his entourage

Sep   Release of an LP, *The Greatest* by Columbia Records

Sep 30   First public mention of Clay in conjunction with the Muslims when the *Philadelphia Daily News* reports that he had attended a 'Black Muslim' rally in Philadelphia

Nov 5   The contract for Clay to fight Sonny Liston is signed

1964

Jan 21   Clay travels to a Muslim rally in New York with Malcolm X and gets up to speak

Jan 24   The result of an Army mental aptitude test gives Clay an IQ score of 78%, below the passing grade for draft

Feb 7   The *Miami Herald* publishes an interview with Cassius Snr, who says his son has joined the 'Black Muslims'

Feb 16   The Beatles come to meet Clay as he trains for the Liston fight in Miami's Fifth Street Gym

Mar 6   Elijah Muhammad announces that he has given Clay the name Muhammad Ali

Mar 26   Ali is reclassified as 1-Y, not qualified for draft under current standards

Apr   Herbert Muhammad becomes part of Ali's entourage

May 14   Ali leaves for a month-long tour of Africa, starting in Ghana then going to Nigeria and finally to Egypt

Jul 3   Herbert Muhammad introduces Ali to Sonji Roi

Aug 14   Ali and Sonji marry in Gary, Indiana

Nov 13   Ali is rushed to hospital for an emergency operation on a hernia

1965

Feb 21   Malcolm X is assassinated

May   Ali appears on the Eamonn Andrews Show on Britain's ATV network

Jun 23   Ali files a complaint to try and annul his marriage to Sonji

mid-year   Bundini is exiled from Ali's entourage for pawning his championship belt

Dec   Ali is presented with the Edward J Neil trophy as 'Fighter of the Year' of 1965, by the Boxing Writers' Association of New York

1966

Jan 10   Ali's divorce from Sonji becomes final

Feb 14   A letter requesting deferment of military service is presented by Ali's lawyer

Feb 17   The request for deferment is denied, and Ali is reclassified 1-A after the required mental aptitude level is lowered

Feb 18   Ali's comment 'I ain't got no quarrel with them Vietcong' is front-page news

Feb 20   The Chicago Tribune calls for sanction of Ali's next bout to be rescinded, following his remark about the Vietcong

Mar 17   Ali appears before the draft board to claim exemption on financial grounds, but also on conscientious-objector status

Aug 23   Ali appears at a special hearing to consider his conscientious-objector status. The hearing officer recommends his claim be sustained

Oct   Ali's contract with the Louisville Sponsoring Group expires, and Herbert Muhammad takes over as his manager

1967

Mar 6   The Appeal Board votes unanimously to maintain Ali's 1-A classification

Apr 28   Muhammad Ali refuses to step forward and be inducted into the US Army

Apr   State Athletic Commissions across America suspend Ali's boxing licence and withdraw recognition of his title

May 8   Ali is indicted by a federal grand jury in Houston, Texas, but is released on $5,000 bail on condition that he does not leave the continental United States

June 19 Beginning of Ali's trial for refusing induction

Aug 17   Ali marries his second wife, Belinda Boyd

1968

May 6   The Fifth Circuit Court of Appeals affirms Ali's conviction

Jun   Ali and Belinda have a daughter, Maryum

Dec   Ali is sent to prison for 10 days, for driving without a valid licence.

1969

Apr 4   The Nation of Islam newspaper, Muhammad Speaks, carries a statement from Elijah Muhammad suspending Ali from membership for saying he wished to box again for money

Aug   Ali and Rocky Marciano film a series of boxing sequences that are then fed into a computer and turned into a fight with the computer predicting the result

Dec   Ali plays the title role in a musical on Broadway, Buck White

1970

           Twins Rasheeda and Jamillah are born to Ali and Belinda

Oct   Bundini is allowed back into Ali's circle

Oct 26   Ali fights his first bout after a three-and-a-half year exile

1971

Jun 28   The United States Supreme Court unanimously reverses Ali's conviction

Oct   Ali goes on a tour of Nigeria, Italy, Switzerland and England, sponsored by Ovaltine

1972

Jan   Ali goes on his first pilgrimage to Makkah

May 14   Muhammad Eban Ali, Ali and Belinda's son, is born in the Women's Medical Hospital in Philadelphia

           Daughter Miya is born, her mother is one of Ali's girlfriends

Autumn Ali opens his training camp at Deer Lake, Pennsylvania

1974

           A daughter, Khaliah, is born to one of Ali's girlfriends

Nov   After visiting France, Ali goes on to England to see Joe Bugner fight

Dec   Ali is named 'Fighter of the Year' by Ring magazine and 'Sportsman of the Year' by Sports Illustrated

1975

Feb 25   Elijah Muhammad dies and his son, Wallace, takes over as leader of the Nation of Islam

Sep   Ali's relationship with Veronica Porche becomes public

1976

Mar 9   UK launch of Ali's 'autobiography', The Greatest, written with Richard Durham and published by Random House

Aug   Veronica and Ali have a daughter, Hana

Sep 2   Belinda and Ali file for divorce

Dec   Ali films his part in the dramatization of *The Greatest*

1977

Jun 19   Ali marries his third wife, Veronica Porche

Aug 12   UK premiere of the film, *The Greatest*, by Columbia Pictures

1978

Feb   Ali goes to Bangladesh and is later appointed Honorary Consul General to the country

Mar   A daughter, Laila, is born to Ali and Veronica

Jun   Ali sets off on a 12-day tour of Moscow, Tashkent and Samarkand

1979

Jan 15   Special showing in London of *Bangladesh I Love You*, which was filmed during Ali's trip the previous year

Jun 26   Ali announces his retirement

          A four-hour mini-series, *Freedom Road*, starring Ali and Kris Kristofferson is aired on American television

1980

Oct 2   Ali returns to the ring to fight Larry Holmes

Dec 18   The film of *Freedom Road* has its UK charity premiere in London

1981

Dec   After his defeat by Trevor Berbick, Ali finally gives up boxing

1984

Sep   Ali is officially diagnosed as suffering from Parkinson's Syndrome

1985

Feb   Ali travels to Beirut to try and negotiate the freedom of four American diplomats

1986

Jul   Veronica and Ali are divorced

Nov 19   Ali marries his fourth wife, Lonnie Williams

1988

          Bundini becomes the first member of the Ali entourage to die

Jul   Ali receives a lifetime achievement award from the United Nations

1990

Nov   Ali travels to Iraq to try to forestall the war. He returns with 15 American hostages.

          Cassius Snr dies

1991

May   Lonnie and Ali adopt a newborn baby boy, who is named Assad Amin

1996

Jul   Ali lights the flame to open the Olympic Games in Atlanta

1999

Oct 8   Laila Ali, daughter of Ali and Veronica, makes her debut as a boxer

Dec   Ali is presented with a 'Sportsman of the Century' trophy by *Sports Illustrated*

2000

Jan 24   The Muhammad Ali Boxing Reform Act is passed by the United States government, to reform unfair and anti-competitive practices in professional boxing

Dec 27   Hollywood stars attend 'An Evening with Muhammad Ali and Friends' to raise funds for a proposed Muhammad Ali Center

2001

Muhammad Ali Center to break ground

2003

Muhammad Ali Center to open

Credits

Pictures in this book are copyright of Associated Newspapers,
except for the following which are copyright of the Hulton Getty Picture Archive.

(T = Top; B = Bottom; L = Left; R = Right):

15 –T; 19; 21; 22; 27 – B; 30 – B; 34; 35 – B; 36 –T + B; 39 –T + B;
40; 41 – B; 49; 50; 52 –T; 53; 56 – B; 58 – B; 59 –T + B;
61 –T + B; 62 –T + B; 63 –T + B; 66; 67 –T + B; 68 –T + B; 72; 73; 75;
77 –T + B; 78 –T + B; 79; 92 – L + R; 93; 99 –T + B;
100 –T; 101- T + B; 102; 103 –T + B; 107 –T; 108 – L; 111 –T + B; 114 –T;
115 – B; 116; 118 –T + B; 119 – B; 122 –T; 127; 128 – B; 129;
130; 131 –T + B; 135; 138 – B; 141 – B; 143; 146; 149 –T + B; 151 –T;
153 – B; 153; 155 –T; 157; 164; 165 –T; 169 – B; 170 –T + B;
172; 173 – B; 175; 177 –T + B; 178; 179; 181 –T + B; 188 –T + B; 189;
190 –T + B; 191 –T; 192 – B; 197 – B; 198 – B; 199;
200 –T + B; 201 –T + BR; 202; 203 – B; 205 –T; 226; 227 –T; 230 – B;
234; 235; 237 –T + B; 238 –T + B; 239 –T + B; 241 –T + B;
242 –T + B; 243 –T + B; 244 –T + B; 245 –T + B; 246 –T + B; 247 –T + B;
248 –T + B; 248; 250; 256 – B; 258; 259; 263 –T; 268; 270 – B;
271 –T + B; 272; 274 –T + B; 285 –T; 288 –T + B; 289; 293 –T; 302; 306 – B;
309 – B; 310 –T; 311 – B; 312 T + B; 313; 314 – B; 315 –TR + B;
320 –T + B; 323 – B; 324

Bibliography

Muhammad Ali, His Life and Times (Pan, London, 1997)
Muhammad Ali, The Eye-witness Story of a Boxing Legend (Carlton, London, 2000)
King of the World (Picador, London, 1999)
The Tao of Muhammad Ali (Vintage, London, 1997)
The Fight (Penguin, London, 2000)